"I THOROUGHLY ENJOYED T
A FAVORITE JAZZ RECORD,
AND OVER AND LEARN M
EACH TIME I READ IT."—Geneva B. Johnson,
President, Family Service America

••

High praise for
best-selling author
Max De Pree
and his extraordinary new work
LEADERSHIP JAZZ

••

"INSIGHTFUL . . . De Pree is adept at identifying the
precise turning points that separate leadership from mere
management."—*The Grand Rapids Press*

"MAX DE PREE HAS A FINE REGARD FOR HIS
READERS—which is in itself a splendid model for great
leadership. He tells us much but not everything: he hints,
he suggests, he nudges, he winks, caps a point with a fine
story and then trusts us to carry the ball for ourselves."
—Dr. Lewis B. Smedes, Professor, Fuller Theological
Seminary

"MAX DE PREE IS RIGHT ON."—Mitchell T. Rabkin,
M.D., Professor of Medicine, Harvard Medical School

"AN ELOQUENT COMPOSITION . . . Reading
De Pree's book is as enjoyable as it is inspiring."
—*Industry Week*

Please turn the page for more extraordinary acclaim . . .

"It is refreshing to read a book about leadership that puts high stock in individual integrity."—*The Christian Science Monitor*

"Once again Max De Pree ignites the language of leadership. 'Polishing gifts,' 'water carriers,' and 'frantic learners' will become a vivid part of tomorrow's management vocabulary and vision. *Leadership Jazz* goes to the top of my list. It is Max De Pree at his best."—Frances Hesselbein, President, Drucker Foundation

••

And praise for
Max De Pree's previous best seller

Leadership Is an Art

••

"THIS IS A WONDERFUL BOOK; it captures Max's spirit—and he's a truly exceptional person. But it also says more about leadership in clearer, more elegant, and more convincing language than many of the much longer books that have been published on the subject."
—Peter F. Drucker

"EVERY MANAGER SHOULD HAVE [THIS BOOK] ON HIS OR HER DESK."—Milton Moskowitz, coauthor of *The 101 Best Companies to Work For in America*

ALSO BY MAX DE PREE

Leadership Is an Art

Max De Pree

Leadership

Jazz

A DELL TRADE PAPERBACK

A DELL TRADE PAPERBACK

Published by
Dell Publishing
a division of
Bantam Doubleday Dell Publishing Group, Inc.
1540 Broadway
New York, New York 10036

ISBN: 0-440-50518-6

Reprinted by arrangement with Doubleday

Printed in the United States of America

Published simultaneously in Canada

October 1993

10 9

For Carl Frost,
a quiet giant who has helped so many
compose voice and touch

Contents

. . . . .

Prologue 1

Finding One's Voice 4

A Key Called Promise 16

What's Fragile? 33

God's Mix 50

Watercarriers 65

Ropes or Bathrooms 76

Leaders' Leaders 93

Take Five 109

What Would Bucky Say? 115

Where Do Ethics and Leadership
Intersect? 125

Give the Gift of Change 140

Delegate! 151

Polishing Gifts 167

Amateurs 185

Followership 197

Do Leaders Have a Future? 207

The Attributes of Leadership:
A Checklist 218

Epilogue 227

LEADERSHIP
JAZZ

Prologue

.....

Esther, my wife, and I have a granddaughter named Zoe, the Greek word for "life." She was born prematurely and weighed one pound, seven ounces, so small that my wedding ring could slide up her arm to her shoulder. The neonatologist who first examined her told us that she had a 5 to 10 percent chance of living three days. When Esther and I scrubbed up for our first visit and saw Zoe in her isolette in the neonatal intensive care unit, she had two IVs in her navel, one in her foot, a monitor on each side of her chest, and a respirator tube and a feeding tube in her mouth.

To complicate matters, Zoe's biological father had jumped ship the month before Zoe was born. Realizing this, a wise and caring nurse named Ruth gave me my instructions. "For the next several months, at least, you're the surrogate father. I want you to come to the hospital every day to visit Zoe, and when you come, I would like you to rub her body and her legs and arms with the tip of your finger. While you're caressing her, you should tell her over and over how much you love her, because she has to be able to connect your voice to your touch."

Ruth was doing exactly the right thing on Zoe's

behalf (and, of course, on my behalf as well), and without realizing it she was giving me one of the best possible descriptions of the work of a leader. At the core of becoming a leader is the need always to connect one's voice and one's touch.

Finding One's
Voice

.....

Ruth was right. Zoe, now a flourishing
four-year-old, and I have a very special
relationship. These days, her voice and
touch are as important to me as my voice
and touch were to her four years ago.
This interdependent relationship, it

seems to me, is one of the results of trying to be a good leader, of composing voice and touch. There is, of course, a prior task—*finding* one's voice in the first place.

One of the ways I have found my own voice over the years is to write. So here is another book, *Leadership Jazz*. I truly hope that it will help you think about the work of leaders, that it will help you in some modest way discover some of the essential elements of leadership. Perhaps more than anything, I hope that together we can ponder the mysterious energy lying impounded in the connection between voice and touch. After all, a leader's voice is the expression of one's beliefs, and the first four chapters especially deal with what we believe. A leader's touch demonstrates competence and resolve, two qualities we can discuss in the rest of the book.

Whether leaders articulate a personal philosophy or not, their behavior surely expresses a personal set of values and beliefs. This holds true for people in businesses and hospitals and colleges and families. The way we build and hold our relationships, the physical settings we produce, the products and services our organizations provide, the way in which we communicate—all of these things reveal who we are. Such is also the case with organizations. General Motors and Exxon have genealogies, personalities, and reputations just as surely as you and I.

Leadership can never stop at words. Leaders must act, and they do so only in the context of their beliefs. Without action or principles, no one can become a leader. This conviction is woven like a red thread through the following chapters.

A great many people in positions of leadership are not waiting around for national or international leaders or for *Fortune* 100 CEOs—or for me —to tell them what to do. They realize that the work of leadership belongs to the thousands of college presidents, hospital board members, people in state and local government, parents and teachers, and people in business organizations large and small. They have already embroiled themselves in the good work of being and becoming leaders. They are eager to equip themselves to do their jobs better.

Leadership is, as you know, not a position but a job. It's hard and exciting and good work. It's also a serious meddling in other people's lives. One examines leadership beginning not with techniques but rather with premises, not with tools but with beliefs, and not with systems but with understandings. This I truly believe.

On a recent trip to England, I looked out of the window just before sunrise as the plane circled over central London on its way to Heathrow. The gauze of a light fog diffused the yellow lights of the city and created a brief but exciting feeling of a new Narnia. I was looking at something I had seen many times before through a new lens.

Leaders need an ability to look through a variety of lenses. We need to look through the lens of a follower. We need to look through the lens of a new reality. We need to look through the lens of hard experience and failure. We need to look through the lens of unfairness and mortality. We need to look hard at our future.

What will be needed by the next generations, our own children and grandchildren? When will we stop being boxed in by national boundaries and cultural stereotypes? What does it mean to modulate individual rights with the common good? Are we ready to make a commitment to civility and inclusiveness? Are we ready to think seriously about a fairer way to distribute economic results among all people? Where will we find new metaphors for these essential ideas?

I enjoy jazz, and one way to think about leadership is to consider a jazz band. Jazz-band leaders must choose the music, find the right musicians, and perform—in public. But the effect of the performance depends on so many things—the environment, the volunteers playing in the band, the need for everybody to perform as individuals and as a group, the absolute dependence of the leader on the members of the band, the need of the leader for the followers to play well. What a summary of an organization!

A jazz band is an expression of servant leadership. The leader of a jazz band has the beautiful opportunity to draw the best out of the other musicians. We have much to learn from jazz-band leaders, for jazz, like leadership, combines the unpredictability of the future with the gifts of individuals.

Leaders certainly need to know where they stand. But *how* do leaders stand? A sound philosophy isn't enough; we all need to connect voice and touch. So much discussion these days talks of ethics as a legal line in the sand, a prohibition against certain actions. But leadership is constructive, the right actions taken in the context of clear and well-considered thinking. The active pursuit of a common good gives us the right to ask leaders and managers of all kinds to be not only successful, but faithful. While measuring success in our society seems to be hardly mysterious enough, judging faithfulness is another matter. After all, a philosophy of leadership or management cannot be caught like a cold.

In an effort to be helpful, let me suggest five criteria as a way to start thinking about faithfulness.

Integrity in all things precedes all else. The open demonstration of integrity is essential; followers must be wholeheartedly convinced of their leaders' integrity. For leaders, who live a public life, perceptions become a fact of life. Leaders understand the profound difference between gestures and commitment. It's just impossible to be a closet leader.

The servanthood of leadership needs to be felt, understood, believed, and practiced if we're to be faithful. The best description of this kind of leadership is found in the book of Luke: "The greatest among you should be like the youngest, and the one who rules, like the one who serves." The finest instruction in how to practice it can be found in *Servant Leadership* by Robert Greenleaf, a lovely grace note to the melody in Luke.

Accountability for others, especially those on the edges of life and not yet experienced in the ways of the world, is one of the great directions leaders receive from the prophet Amos. Amos tells us that leaders should encourage and sustain those on the bottom rung first and then turn to those on the top. Should we call this the trickle-up theory?

There is a great misconception in organizations: that a manager must be either in control or not in control. The legitimate alternative is *the practice of equity*. This is surely a reasonable component in anyone's philosophy of management. While equity should certainly guide the apportioning of resources, it is far more important in our human relationships. (See "A Key Called Promise" for more about equity.)

The last criterion for faithfulness (in this list, that is; of course you will think of more) is that leaders have to be *vulnerable*, have to offer others the opportunity to do their best. Leaders become vulnerable by sharing with others the marvelous gift of being personally accountable. People in a capitalist system become vulnerable by creating a genuine opportunity for others to reach their potential at the same time that all work together toward corporate goals.

In finding one's voice and connecting it to one's touch, three questions come to mind: "What shall I promise?" "Can the so-called bottom line truly be the bottom line?" and "Who speaks for whom?" I hope you'll find your answers somewhere in this book.

You've recently been promoted. You're now a vice president or a provost or a department supervisor. Now the work begins. You haven't arrived, you've only begun to travel. In the same way, having children means only that the work of becoming a parent has begun. The biological event is very different from the love and commitment, the skinned knees and dirty diapers, the faithfulness to homework and Little League, the sacrifices for tuition and music lessons, the laughter and the tears—these kinds of things add up to earning the title "Mom" or "Dad."

One becomes a leader, I believe, through doing the work of a leader. It's often difficult and painful and sometimes even unrewarding, and it's work. There are also times of joy in the work of leadership, and doing the work of a leader is necessary in our society.

I hope that *Leadership Jazz* offers you some clues as to how leaders might act and what kind of thinking might precede action, whether you're parent or teacher, president or supervisor, preacher or member of Congress. I hope that reading this book will encourage you to see the breadth and depth of potential that exists in the work of every leader. I hope that you, too, will discover that so much of leadership is music from the heart.

Books that explain everything give only the author's point of view and leave little room for a reader to elaborate and connect and interpret through her own experiences and background. I have left room in *Leadership Jazz* for you to complete this book. I hope that you will read and write between the lines and improve what I have done. Authors and leaders who see only a limited need for the gifts of followers limit themselves to their own talents. I have tried to make this book inviting, but to complete the ideas may require a serious effort on your part.

I am not here as someone who has everything figured out but rather as one who struggles. I can't answer every question about leadership. The story goes that a German machine tool company once developed a very fine bit for drilling holes in steel. The tiny bit could bore a hole about the size of a human hair. This seemed like a tremendously valuable innovation. The Germans sent samples off to Russia, the United States, and Japan, suggesting that this bit was the ultimate in machining technology.

From the Russians, they heard nothing. From

the Americans came a quick response inquiring as to the price of the bits, available discounts, and the possibility of a licensing arrangement.

After some delay, there was the predictable, polite response from the Japanese, complimenting the Germans on their achievement, but with a postscript noting that the Germans' bit was enclosed with a slight alteration. Excitedly, the German engineers opened the package, carefully examined their bit, and to their amazement discovered that the Japanese had bored a neat hole through it.

A Key Called Promise

. . . . .

"I have a key in my bosom, called Promise, that will, I am persuaded, open any lock in Doubting Castle."

—*The Pilgrim's Progress*

Leadership may be good work, but it's also a tough job. There is always more to do than time seems to allow. Measuring out both time to pursue one's own responsibilities and time to respond to the needs of others can be difficult. And leaders are constantly under pressure to make promises.

Though I'm still learning things about being a leader, I can tell you at least two requirements of such a position: the need to give one's witness as a leader—to make your promises to the people who allow you to lead; and the necessity of carrying out your promises. It sounds easier than it is.

One day Pat McNeal, a scheduler in the plant whom I'd known for a good many years, called me to say that Valerie from the second shift wanted to talk to me about a very serious matter. At the time I was CEO. Not knowing me, she had asked Pat to pave the way into my office. Pat said, "I want you to know that Valerie's a very dependable person. You would be wise to listen to what she has to say."

A date was set and Valerie appeared. She began by asking me if I knew that a vice president had fired the relatively new manager of the second shift without following the prescribed procedures. I told her that no, I wasn't aware of this. She then gave me the entire story of the abrupt and unwarranted dismissal of not one, but two fine young managers of the second and third shifts by this vice president, who seemed to have lost his bearings.

Valerie then handed me a beautifully written petition outlining the qualifications of the second-shift manager, his performance, and his relationship with all the people on the shift. Every person on the second shift had signed.

Those of you who have had experience managing in manufacturing plants will understand the risk Valerie ran in circulating the petition and in coming to me. The careful investigation that followed proved Valerie and her co-workers entirely correct and demonstrated that Valerie was serving Herman Miller (our company) well by protesting the firings. Valerie—not her superior in the hierarchy—was honoring corporate values and policies. She had put me and other senior managers in the position of living up to policies the company had clearly promised. Valerie was helping the leaders of the company to connect voice and touch.

Many of us privately make promises. We promise ourselves to lose weight, work harder, or finish a book. If we don't keep this kind of promise, we can usually find a reason, sometimes even a good reason. But followers can't afford leaders who make casual promises. Someone is likely to take them seriously. Leaders make public promises. They put themselves on the line to the people they lead. An enormous chasm separates the private world, where we often smile indulgently at broken promises, from the public one, where unkept promises do great harm. Leaders constantly look out across the distance. For no leader has the luxury of making a promise in a vacuum.

At no time is the gap between individual needs and organizational needs more painfully obvious than in times of cutbacks or difficult business conditions. Leaders must balance sensitively the needs of people and of the institution. A leader's promises come under critical examination at these times. A leader who backs away from her promises under duress irreparably damages the organization and plants the seeds of suspicion among her followers.

What would happen if the President of the United States were to visit an inner-city Chicago elementary school, tell the teachers and administration that she was publicly taking accountability for improving that school, and promise that she would hold the administration and teachers accountable? And, the President would continue, "I will visit this school exactly one year from now to see what progress has been made. Call me for help." Does anyone doubt that the quality of education in the school would rise?

There is great power in the public promise of a true leader, power to strengthen and enable people. One of the great dangers to organizations arises when a leader's private and public promises contradict each other. Then the expectations of followers are liable to go beyond the reality delivered. Especially in lively, exciting institutions and corporations, when the private and public worlds of the leaders become confounded or contradictory, the mix-up can be deadly. At this point, we begin to question the leader's integrity.

Another of the great problems of leadership is what exactly to promise. The clarity and appropriateness of a leader's promises bear directly on the effectiveness and maturity of the institution and the performance of the people in it. What should a leader take from the private and personal bouts of concentrated thinking about the institution's future and make public as a promise?

The best leaders promise only what's worth defending.

With this in mind, before looking at what a leader may promise, I would like to discuss a few givens essential when thinking about leadership.

It's important to understand that good work means something a little different these days. In today's workplace, where the great majority of people are well prepared and thoroughly motivated, individual involvement through an open, participative structure or system of management most often elicits good performance. Every vital organization thrives because it depends more on commitment and enthusiasm than on the letter of the contract.

Because of the variety of gifts and skills that people bring to the workplace, the need for good people, and their willingness to move, we should treat the great majority of people as volunteers. They don't have to stay in one place. They don't have to work for one company or for one leader. They follow someone only when she deserves it. Thus leaders and followers don't sit on parallel lines, always close but never meeting. Leaders and followers are all parts of a circle.

Whether formally or informally, it's important to recognize that practically everything we accomplish happens through teamwork. We are not on our own. Everyone works within a loop of social accountabilities—a family, a congregation, a business. Ours is an arm-in-arm accountability.

The highest-risk leader is the one who thinks she works alone.

It's important to understand that leadership is a posture of indebtedness. The process of leading is the process of fulfilling commitments made both to persons and to the organization. A leader's promises are her commitments. Keeping these promises and the way in which they are kept are parts of the mystery and the art of leadership. Knowing what not to do is fully as important as knowing what to do.

Followers really determine how successful a leader will be. And so I would like to propose some ways of thinking about followership. What are the rights and needs of followers? Remember to think of followers as volunteers. Remember, too, that the goals of the organization are best met when the goals of people in the organization are met at the same time. These two sets of goals are seldom the same. While teaching at night school, I used to ask my classes, "Why do you go to work?" No one ever answered, "To make profit for the company."

Any follower has a right to ask many things of her leader. Here are several questions that leaders should expect to hear. The answers to these questions, you see, are some of the promises leaders will make.

- What may I expect from you?
- Can I achieve my own goals by following you?
- Will I reach my potential by working with you?
- Can I entrust my future to you?
- Have you bothered to prepare yourself for leadership?
- Are you ready to be ruthlessly honest?
- Do you have the self-confidence and trust to let me do my job?
- What do you believe?

Some time ago, shortly after the board of directors had elected Ed Simon president and chief operating officer of Herman Miller, I was out in one of our plants. A longtime worker stopped me and wanted to talk about the reasons for, and the implications of, this important decision. He had a number of well-thought-out questions, and I could tell that he had been waiting for me to come by. Without thinking, I started to answer some of his questions. I was foolish enough to think that the chairman of the board knew all the answers! He interrupted me. "I don't want to hear you answer these questions, I need to hear Ed's answers. I already know that Ed is our new president, but what I need to know is, *who is Ed?*" And he wasn't asking what Ed looked like.

This person needed to know what kind of a leader he was following and what this new leader would promise.

What a leader promises to the institution can be developed by thinking in a certain way about the needs of the institution. Just as individuals have a right to expect certain things of a leader, an institution (as a corporate body of many groups of people) expects and demands certain things from its leaders. I will list a few to stimulate your thinking.

(You'll notice that I haven't listed the promises leaders should make. I can't tell you that. The promises that come from a leader tell the story of her mettle. How those promises are carried out reveals the position a leader will occupy in the history of the organization.)

The organization expects the leader to define and express both in writing and, especially, through behavior the beliefs and values of the institution. This may not be easy, but like many disciplines, it's essential. Writing down what an institution values makes everyone come clean. It can also make people uncomfortable. The safety of vaguely known beliefs will disappear pretty fast.

To carry out its work, the organization needs from a leader a clear statement of its vision and its strategy. Of course, a leader may not be the only author of these, but she is primarily accountable for expressing them and making them understood.

A leader is accountable for the design of the busi-

ness. A business or institutional structure, the bones and muscle of any organization, needs always to be kept in sync with the strategy and aimed at the future. The design of the organization should never be gerrymandered to serve the politicians or the bureaucracy of the insiders.

A leader is responsible for lean and simple statements of policy consistent with beliefs and values, vision and strategy. Policy gives practical meaning to values. Policies must actively enable people whose job it is to carry them out. I'm not talking about rules here. Leaders who live by rules rather than by principles are no more than dogs in mangers.

Equity is the special province of a leader. There is more than the financial side of equity, and I do not mean control. A leader is responsible for equity in the assignment of all resources, tangible and intangible, in relation to agreed-on priorities. I hope that you will allow me to include in the meaning of equity the chance to advance in the organization and the chance to reach one's potential. I would also put in this definition communication, recognition, and reward. Any organization accrues to itself these three kinds of equity. It is incumbent on a leader to protect them.

A leader focuses not on her own image as leader, but on the tone of the body of the institution. Followers, not leaders, accomplish the work of the organization. We need to be concerned, therefore, with how the followers deal with change. How do they handle a customer's need for good service and good quality? How do the followers deal with conflict? How do they measure and respond to their results? These are questions that will help us evaluate the tone of the body; these are the ways in which the work of a leader comes under scrutiny. Just how lithe is your organization?

Appearance follows substance; the message subordinates the medium. A leader gets good results by leading, not by appearing to lead. The Marquis de Custine, a French traveler, was crossing with a group of Russian nobles from Sweden to St. Petersburg in the nineteenth century. The

Russians were discussing the burdens of attending at the Czar's court, among which was the obligation to listen politely to all sorts of trivial and boring conversation. They were trying to determine the best way of appearing to listen, since we all admire attentiveness. The Frenchman made a simple observation. "The best way of appearing to listen," he said, "is to listen."

A leader ensures that priorities are set, that they are steadfastly communicated and adhered to in practice. This can be accomplished only if the leader halts the endless negotiation of the politicians in the group, the negotiators' waltz, as I sometimes call it. The participative process stimulates contrary opinion, as it should, but no organization can survive endless negotiation. At some point, public acceptance of a direction must appear.

A leader ensures that the planning for the organization at all levels receives the necessary direction and approvals. The benefits of a good plan are threefold. It sets a clear direction. It makes the necessary objectives and goals visible and understandable. It serves as a road map for all the people in the organization who need to know where and with whom to make a connection.

A leader reviews and assesses results primarily in three areas: key appointments and promotions, results compared to the plan, the connections to key publics. Promotions, key appointments, and succession planning are the most crucial elements in the organization's future. These activities are a leader's true domain. The organization has a right to understand the criteria used in these decisions, and each one must be examined carefully.

One of the many pacts of love that a leader upholds is to make the organization accountable for results compared to the plan. Not to be accountable for results is to be seriously out of touch with reality. Only leaders can stand up to the organization and hold it to its goals and to its required performance.

Institutions must never be permitted to operate in isolation. It is a matter of survival that we stay in touch with reality by opening ourselves to key groups: students and faculty, followers and customers, constituents and stockholders. Perhaps only success is more fragile in institutional life than the condition of being truly in touch with what's real.

Leaders are accountable for the continuous renewal of the organization. Renewal, I think, results directly when a leader understands and communicates opportunities, constraints, and reality. The understanding without communication is futile; communication without understanding is fruitless. Leaders need a solid understanding, and they owe pellucid explanation. We also need to remember that the unexamined message is not worth giving. The leader who opens her communication to question and debate brings about a much more promising result. If you believe this, it's easy to see that video reports are not communications.

Renewal also requires that leaders be alive in a special way to innovation and be hospitable to the creative person. This brings an ability to solve problems, to deal constructively with change, and to enable and encourage continual personal growth.

A leader ought never to embarrass followers. What is it exactly that embarrasses one's followers? Just ask them.

Leaders can only do so much. In very small organizations, leaders can sometimes have a hand in everything. This soon changes. In larger organizations, leaders simply can't do the work that moves the group day to day. Nor should they. Leaders remain responsible, perhaps more so than anyone else, for making the future promising and making promises for the future.

Businesses and institutions, like nature, abhor a vacuum. A leader who makes no promises leaves a vacuum soon to be filled by promises made by other people for her or by politicians trying to manipulate the organization. The best leaders make their promises under the public scrutiny of their followers. Then they keep them. This is one way to connect voice and touch.

What's
Fragile?
.....

Believe it or not, one of a leader's chief concerns is the problem of betrayal. Many kinds of betrayals take place in organizations. Authors and editors may betray each other; architects and builders may betray each other.

Leaders often betray followers and vice versa. Most betrayals come to light after the fact, after one party silently abandons a goal or a commitment.

Betrayal is closely linked to the idea of entropy, the tendency of everything to deteriorate. Both have a way of sneaking up on us. Both hover constantly over organizations, waiting for the slightest slackening of our vigilance. Neither results especially from poor motivation or outright sabotage. Rather, they seem to me to creep into organizations when a leader fails to reflect seriously on what makes important things go awry. Slothful people allow entropy to ruin things; leaders are directly responsible for the very existence of betrayal.

From a leader's perspective, the most serious betrayal has to do with thwarting human potential, with quenching the spirit, with failing to deal equitably with each other as human beings.

The fragile aspects in the life of a leader and an organization are always most liable to be betrayed.

To answer the question in the title of this chapter, I have talked to people with the special gift of being at the heart of an organization—not the center. CEOs and members of Congress and deans, by the nature of the power that accumulates around them, are at the center. They can't avoid it. Being at the center, being in control, differs from being at the heart. People with the special gift of being at the heart (and there are some rare and wonderful instances where a person is both at the center and at the heart) have an exotic perspective. Leaders can learn from these people, who see the diversity in organizations and understand how to take advantage of it. They affirm good values. They understand the role of high-quality relationships. They know that significant change requires a form of dying.

I have spent some time with these people at the heart of things, and I'd like to tell you what they think is fragile in the lives of leaders. I can tell you that making a list like this of the findings of my rather amateurish research was possible only after listening arduously and accurately. Then I had to summon the courage and honesty to deal with the implications. You will have more to add to this list, I hope.

Beliefs and values are the footings on which we build answers to the questions "Who matters?" and "What matters?" The promises we make as leaders must resonate with our beliefs and values. Otherwise they ring false, and people know it. In our lives as leaders, we frequently find ourselves in situations where skill and technique fail us. At times professional qualifications simply aren't enough. We need to resort to deeper resources, resources beyond technique and the jargon of seminars, resources rooted in our beliefs and values.

It behooves us, then, to find our voices. Leaders must speak to followers; we must let them know where and how we stand on the important issues. We constantly make decisions and evaluate results in light of what we believe.

A medieval story will let you know what I

mean about actions illustrating belief. Envy and
Greed, two of the seven deadly sins, were walking
down a path one day when they were confronted
by an angel. The angel offered one of them everything he could wish for. The other one would
receive twice as much. Greed quickly asked Envy
to choose first. After a little thought, Envy wished
for one blind eye.

Leaders can be, when they choose, significant bear-
ers of gifts to the spirit. There are many kinds of
gifts to the spirit. Louis Armstrong was one. So is
Itzhak Perlman, with the beautiful talent he has
and with the elegant way in which he exercises it.

There was at Herman Miller a department supervisor to whom many disabled people seemed to
gravitate. This supervisor seemed to have a way of
providing a place for them. I once asked him why
this was. He answered very simply, "Max, it's just
a matter of letting people know how much we
need them." Howard is a real gift to the spirit.

Leaders understand that reaching one's potential is a mysterious thing, something that often

takes place outside of a leader's control or direction. A sign of true leadership is a feeling of freedom among followers to stage a musical or start a band, to play a joke or pull a prank—activities that a leader sometimes never sees and of which a leader is, and isn't, a part. Leaders are often sadly isolated from the small, vital bursts of spirit that sparkle in healthy organizations.

Several years ago, Esther and I and our daughter Nancy attended a Thanksgiving service at Herman Miller's main plant. After the service, a number of the younger guys on the third shift stopped to say hello, and several of them wanted to meet Nancy. A couple of the young men invited us to come back at 1 A.M. for their traditional Thanksgiving dinner. "It will be catered in at the west end of the building. If you can join us, we'd surely like that," they said. "But please don't tell our third-shift manager. He's new on the job and doesn't yet know that these things go on."

Leaders understand and recognize the need to serve; they give their service to people who choose to follow them. Leaders understand Robert Greenleaf when he writes about that curious and wonderful idea of "servant leadership." Leaders understand the role of community and its bearing on the effectiveness of a group. Leaders understand the importance of beauty and permanence and continuity in organized life.

If we ignore these passions or fail to communicate or express them, we do so at great risk. Organizations do not live on earnings alone.

A leader's poise is fragile. Yet how important the quality of poise is to followers. Who feels comfortable following a leader unprepared in difficult circumstances or ill at ease in happy ones?

One element of poise is surely the ability to take everyone seriously. For everyone is equally authentic and surrounded by the mystery of potential. Organizations simply can't survive without all kinds of people. My mother once remarked to me, "I'm getting older, and I can't walk so fast anymore. But you can walk more slowly."

Vision is the basis for the best kind of leadership. A

vision exists somewhere when teams succeed. In-stinctively, most of us follow a leader who has real vision and who can transform that vision into a meaningful and hopeful strategy. I'm not talking here about next quarter's sales targets—that is no vision. But the tenders of visions are often lonely, usually unpopular, and frequently demand that others change. People with a vision inject ambi-guity and risk and uncertainty into our lives. They embark on voyages to new worlds. Without the vitality and strength of an organization, a vision wastes away. How often do you suppose that mag-nificent visions are rendered ineffectual by the failure of the leader to communicate that vision to the people able to realize it?

Fragility is part of a vision's nature. People who think they have created an indestructible vision simply issue a command, write an agenda. Had Odysseus sailed home according to an agenda, the account of his voyage would not be worth remem-bering.

Certain facets of a leader's character are especially fragile. Truth, patience, love, and commitment are examples. You can extend the list. Consistency, one of the highest expectations we have of leaders, is constantly open to compromise. Certain understandings between leaders and followers are fragile: the understanding, for example, that real participation is a process of becoming and never arriving.

Another fragile facet of a leader's character is what I call an eagerness for the fray. The best leaders I know are always anxious to get to the job at hand, to do what they are there to do. You'd never want to go to sea with a captain who would rather be in port.

Vulnerability in a leader enables others to do their best and to be fully accountable. And, of course, being vulnerable to the strengths of other people also makes a leader vulnerable to their weaknesses. To me, this is simply part of being human. A business student asked me one day if there were such a thing as safe vulnerability. Questions like that worry me more than frontal assaults.

We must always be aware of the preparation for leadership. I have had a number of experiences with people who yearned for the responsibilities of leadership, who had the necessary gifts, but who failed to understand the need to be personally prepared. Preparation for leadership is a clear debt to followers and the organization. From the followers' point of view, it is an indispensable expectation.

There are no shortcuts to preparing for leadership. The accretion of layers of skill takes time. Polishing one's gifts requires the tumbling of experience and the grit of great discipline. Learning to identify the needs of followers and the special process of reaching simultaneously toward the potential of individuals and of the organization does not come easy. Failure is an unavoidable part of this preparation.

Preparation for leadership does not come from

books. Books sometimes give you an insight or an outline, but real preparation consists of hard work and wandering in the desert, of much feedback, much forgiveness, and of the yeast of failure. Believe me, it's a lot like learning to hit a curveball —a fragile and fleeting business.

Moving up in the hierarchy does not confer competence. This is hard to keep in mind. The entire metaphor of hierarchy, of moving up the ladder, lures many people into the trap of believing that position equals ability. Careful observers of businesses, colleges, and families—especially people at the heart of these groups—have witnessed over and over the heartache and havoc, strain and stupidity, brought on by the foolish notion that a promotion invariably increases one's competence. Many people honestly believe that a promotion or change in status instantly and mystically qualifies them to handle any problem that comes their way or that they may seek out. Nothing could be further from the truth.

A promotion likely to pan out produces temporary incompetence, the kind of awkwardness that always comes before deeper understanding. The only appropriate response to a promotion is "Good grief, have I got a lot to learn now!"

An organization's cultural harmony is fragile. I'm talking about the sweet music that emanates from diverse and productive groups of people. Leaders certainly have a hand in creating the atmosphere where this kind of harmony can exist, but they don't direct it or mandate it or control it. By harmony, I don't mean homogeneity.

Creating this atmosphere is certainly a central part of the good work of leadership. It begins with the attitude of a leader and grows stronger through a leader's actions. (See "God's Mix" for more about this subject.)

An institution's future is fragile. What ensures it? A number of things, each of them fragile—every promotion, every decision related to changes in leadership, the degree to which leaders balance the forces of change and continuity. Annual plans or strategic initiatives do not guarantee an institu-

44

tion's future; they may even betray it by blinding the organization to other goals. Every key job assignment, every missed opportunity for development, every person inspired by a true leader—these are the things that actually shape the future. I'm talking about the quality of relationships and the enabling of other people.

Closely related to this idea are the problems that surface when we lose sight of who we are and why we are here. Leaders cannot afford to lose track of the present. I often think of the apostolic zeal of leaders like Mohandas Gandhi and Albert Schweitzer. They knew where they stood and where they wanted to go and, especially, who they needed to be.

A few questions about the present will give you a good idea of how fragile the future of institutions really is. How hospitable are you to an innovative idea? Do you really welcome and consider contrary opinions and dissenting perceptions? (I don't mean that patronizing smile and nod of people who have already made up their minds.) How open are you really to the surprise of innovation and the sting of the unfamiliar? How open is your group to new blood? Are you friendly and helpful, or are you out for the kill? Add your own questions. They are the forms and shapes of the future, each as likely to disappear as to become reality.

The health of the organization is fragile. Who are the mentors that encourage and support people in our institution? It is a crucial and tenuous matter, the identifying of people who bring health to the organization and to its leaders. Once you have identified the health-givers, naturally you ask yourself how to nurture that relationship. Am I, too, a health-giver? We can measure our own aptitude at giving health by watching the people truly skilled at it.

The company I work for, like a lot of corporations, maintains a jet. We use it mainly to fly potential customers to our headquarters in Michigan. On one trip, Bill Caudill, a member of our board for years, was to fly in this jet. As he walked out to the plane, he was greeted by Ed Martin, one of the pilots. Bill abruptly, but in a friendly way, asked to see Ed's license. Ed showed it to Bill, and the flight proceeded.

Ed told me this story five years after it happened. It was the only time anyone had ever asked Ed to see his license. "Max," Ed said to me, "I don't know why I wasn't angry or insulted. But this was something I'll never forget. It made me realize that my job was important and Bill Caudill knew that." This is what I mean by health-giving.

There is one last thing on my list of fragile qualities of leadership—success. *Success can expose us to dangerous consequences.* A kind of paradoxical claim to make about something we all reach for, yet it's true. Everybody battles for success; too few people are aware of its profound impact. Success tends to breed arrogance, complacency, and isolation. Success can close a mind faster than prejudice. Success is fragile, like a butterfly. We usually crush the life out of it in our efforts to possess it.

*   *   *

These are some of the things I have learned from people at the heart of organizations. Leaders are fragile precisely at the point of their strengths, liable to fail at the height of their success. A leader's ability to be faithful, especially in relation to the vision and strategy of the institution, is a perpetually open question. We see that leaders are fragile in a special way in the quality of their relationships and, therefore, in the impact they will surely have on the ability of their followers to reach their potential.

To be aware of the fragile elements of leadership is to take an important step toward personal effectiveness and inclusive leadership. To admit that each of us has fragile parts of our lives in institutions is to build stronger relationships.

It's common to think of the strength and power inherent in the position of CEO or provost or director. If the people who fill these positions become true leaders, I'm convinced that the fragility of their position will dawn on them.

In a way, leadership is as delicate as Mozart's

melodies. The music exists and it doesn't. It is written on the page, but it means nothing until performed and heard. Much of its effect depends on the performer and the listener. The best leaders, like the best music, inspire us to see new possibilities.

God's Mix

. . . . .

1. Her name is Carla, handsome, mother of twin boys. She drove a lift truck on the second shift. She came into my office with a ten-ounce paper cup of Coke, made herself comfortable, and told me about her family's vacation trip from

Michigan to Florida when she was a little girl.

The story hinged on one event. "We were driving through a county in one of the Deep South states," she said. "My father was wearing his white cowboy hat. It seemed like I never saw my father without his cowboy hat. A deputy sheriff stopped our car. In those days, we knew that black people should not roll down the windows or unlock the doors at a time like this. The deputy rapped his nightstick hard on the window next to my dad's head and said to him loud enough for all of us to hear, 'Boy, when you're in this county, you drive with your hat off.' My dad put his hat on the seat beside him and left it there until we passed the county line. I made up my mind then that I would always speak up against that kind of treatment."

We talked some more together, and Carla told me that the minority program at our main plant was not going as well as I thought it was. Carla could not let some of the incidents go unprotested. I was flattered and humbled that she had come to me. She had taken the first and most difficult step. So I asked Carla what she wanted me to do. She said, "You're the CEO. It's your job to tell us what you believe." I said, "Fine, I'll do that."

In our time together, Carla helped me see the sacred nature of personal dignity.

2. Many years earlier, Egbert, a master upholsterer in our chair plant, came to me about his sister Betty. Betty had a slight physical disability and had been unable, after months of searching, to find work. Egbert proposed to me that we give Betty a chance. He would give me his guarantee. No charity. We would pay her exactly what she was worth. He promised that she would arrive every day on time, work a full day, and be productive. He would train her and guide Betty's supervisor. No charity, just a chance.

As I listened to Egbert, I realized that here was a man intimate with the pain and despair of being different. He understood Betty's difficulty in finding where she could make her contribution. Egbert made me understand that the mystery around potential is so great that even the most perceptive of us cannot look at a person and decide for certain whether or not she'll be good at this or that, whether or not she'll become a sales manager or vice president—or even the best shortstop you ever saw. We really should be in awe of human potential.

3. *One time in a Phoenix hotel, my left knee gave out, and I was unable to walk.* A visit to the local emergency room produced only a pair of crutches, no real solution. The hotel where Esther, my wife, and I were staying provided me a wheelchair, and the next morning Esther and I appeared in the restaurant for breakfast, Esther pushing me in my wheelchair.

We had eaten several meals in the restaurant, and each time the hostess had looked at me and asked politely the same question, "How many?"

Not this morning. She looked right past me to Esther and said politely, "How many?" Then as she led us into the dining room, she turned again to Esther and asked, "Would he like to sit at the window?"

I had disappeared. In a twinkling, this polite, well-meaning young woman had stripped me of identity and position. It made me realize that to be oppressed is wrong, but to be overlooked may be even worse.

4. *To win a Frost Award at Herman Miller, you have to be named an outstanding employee by your peers.* Then the senior management team must select you as one of two or three outstanding contributors in the entire company. It is a real honor and now carries with it a five-thousand-dollar stipend for continuing education. One can go to school for a period in London or Lausanne or São Paulo. Many have.

Manuel had won a Frost Award and came to ask me if he could use the money in a different way. He was still commuting every weekend from Mexico to our Irvine, California, plant and was enduring the separation every work week from his wife and four children. His goal was to immigrate to the United States. He told me that before the family immigrated, he wanted each of his children to be fluent in English. He wanted to use the stipend for language lessons for his children.

Naturally we agreed. I was reminded in a touching way that rewards and recognition are not the same for all of us.

These four brief stories have moved me beyond diversity, beyond pluralism, to a new perspective on human strength and potential, perhaps the largest resource available to a leader. Groups unavoidably encompass diverse people, thank goodness.

As I reflect on these incidents spread out over thirty-five years, I ask myself: What do I really believe about Carla and Betty and Manuel? How can a leader interpret lessons like these—experiences that are the raw materials of understanding? These people and their stories are not extraordinary in today's society. They're commonplace. These people are neighbors and co-workers. As an article in *The Economist* pointed out to me, the 1980s saw the largest numbers ever of immigrants to the United States. By the middle of the next century, perhaps fewer than half of all Americans will be white. More than half of children in California's schools today are nonwhite. This carries important implications for leaders.

The human need for dignity and opportunity and reward must move us beyond the stiff and bureaucratic language of governmental regulations. It seems to me that such regulations, as necessary as they are, form only the most basic and generalized statement of fair behavior. They are the least risky involvement. Hiding behind the approved vocabulary—EEOC, barrier-free, affirmative action—prevents us from seeing in a clear-eyed way that this is an issue of the heart. Antoine de Saint-Exupéry put it elegantly. "It is only with the heart that one can see rightly; what is essential is invisible to the eye."

We are not talking simply about diversity, or rights, or compliance. Leaders are required to understand that this is a much deeper matter, a matter of authenticity. We are dealing with the elements of human worth.

We are dealing with God's mix, people made in God's image, a compelling mystery.

Each of us is part of the same family. Each of us is an ingredient in a great, cross-cultural mix. Each of us is an essential atom in a living, breathing, and changing organism. Each of us has beauty, potential, and rights. We are all authentic in our own right; no person awards us authenticity; we are born with it.

If you agree with me so far, I think you will find our perspective lends an elegant clarity to this issue. It enables us to see into the heart of things. We can exchange suspicion for vulnerability. We can exchange the superficial for the substantive. We can exchange the shifting ground of tactics for the solid ground of understanding. We can exchange arm's-length relationships for shoulder-to-shoulder unity. We can exchange judgment for acceptance. We can welcome with open arms everything that these exchanges imply for our attitude and behavior. We can follow belief with example. We can compose our voice and touch.

So how, in this matter, are leaders to do good work? What kind of perspective can true leaders bring to the issue of authenticity?

Let me suggest a few ideas. You will surely think of more.

First, I think leaders see our institutions, our families, our corporations, cross-culturally. The emphasis here is on the verb *see.* We, our families, corporations, and institutions together, form a colorful and diverse pageant of individuals and groups searching for ways to contribute and to become what we are not now. There is no one, single costume.

Next, leaders understand that this intense mixture is legitimate and has meaning and belongs. To realize this in one's heart is not easy. It means opening ourselves to the eccentricities, the weaknesses—*and, therefore, the strengths*—of other people.

Then leaders affirm that authenticity is a matter of the heart and, thus, an issue of limitless depth and potential. It is not an issue to be resolved by legislation or manuals. Leaders will plumb the depths of human authenticity, perhaps without ever reaching the bottom.

From this understanding and perspective, leaders can begin to act. For leaders, there can be no disjunction between thought and action. One of a leader's chief responsibilities is to initiate action. Leaders can then help people respond in a way that honors the personal dignity of everyone and that gives each person the space to be what she can be.

This kind of leadership calls for guidelines. Here are mine. Leaders:

- Try to see that we all tend to be intolerant. Intolerance extends to the shy and the gregarious, to the attractive and the unattractive, to the overweight and the slim.

- Understand that people only listen to preaching; they emulate behavior.

- Accept risk. This is terribly hard to do, for I am constantly aware that when I as a leader take on a risk, I am introducing risk into the lives of other people. The necessity and potential in accepting risks are self-evident.

- Provide a measure of grace as the antidote to the behavior of people who poison our society with disgrace.

- Accept the normal accountability for bringing about change.

- Don't apologize for the truth.

- Think clearly about the role of nuance in the way they are perceived.

- Make their organizations big enough to be natural for all the different kinds of people who work there. By "big enough," I'm not talking about the number of employees or the size of buildings. People need to feel free enough to be naturally who they are.

- Remember that believing in the authenticity of people is real and workable. Such a belief is patently right.

- Live with reality. Even enjoy it. It's part of the world. People do take drugs. The real question is, now what?

- Are impatient! Are patient! Leaders, no matter how committed, cannot prescribe a quick cure for bigotry or prejudice. The cure begins when we connect the heart and the mind, the voice and the touch. Leaders will make progress simply by seeing the authenticity in individuals and making sure individuals know that they publicly acknowledge it. Then leaders must hold other people —as well as themselves—accountable.

- Make a long-term commitment.

If we work at this, what results may we dream of? Let me start to describe my dream. You can create your own between the lines. Here are the results I see growing from these seeds.

- The leader's public acknowledgment of the authenticity of each and every person. (Are you willing to make this one of your promises?)

- Advocacy. At Herman Miller we have a vice president for people. Notice that the title is *for* people, not *of* people. A true advocate.

- Civility in our organizations.

- Hope. The failure of leaders to supply hope lies at the heart of the predicament in which so many young people find themselves. Steeling oneself to become what one is not requires hope. Leaders can give it.

- Health. And I don't mean a cure for the common cold. I mean the health that springs from hope and leads to results and performance.

- Fairness—not only in a legal sense. We must take a new look in America at the distribution of results. Capitalism must become inclusive in all regards.

- Renewal.

How might a sincere effort in this direction affect a leader? It can only make one a more effective agent of doing good work. There is, you see, a real beauty in God's mix. By accepting our responsibilities as leaders in that mix, we can uncover the secret to our own individual maturity and potential. We can derive strength from our human bonds rather than building walls out of human differences. We are personally incomplete, inchoate, in our lonely, isolated state. We need to become submerged in this mix if we are to move in the direction of wholeness. Our fulfillment in life depends on this wholeness.

As in a lasting marriage, the kind of belief and behavior I'm talking about is not a matter of charity. It isn't now, nor will it be, a luxury for corporations, colleges, or churches. It results from hard work and open hearts. Any organization seeking to progress, to produce, will be required to live up to the potential lying hidden in its diversity.

We need to commit ourselves to individual authenticity with openness and expectation, with grace and humor. We need to drop our guards. We need to leap into a faith in authenticity as children leap from the side of a swimming pool into their parent's arms. I truly believe that there lies within us a creative love. If we let it creep out, I'm convinced we'll be overwhelmed by the response.

In a society and a world that have serious problems and suffer all too often and far too painfully from heartbreak, each of us needs a haven. Part of the touch of leadership is to create such a haven. A good family, a good institution, or a good corporation can be a place of healing. It can be a place where work becomes redemptive, where every person is included on her own terms. We know in our hearts that to be included is both beautiful and right. Leaders have to find a way to work that out, to contribute toward that vision.

Watercarriers

.....

The tribal watercarrier in this corporation is a symbol of the essential nature of all jobs, our interdependence, the identity of ownership and participation, the servanthood of leadership, the authenticity of each individual.

—Inscription next to the Watercarrier
sculpture at Herman Miller's
corporate headquarters

In the life of an American Indian tribe, the watercarrier held one of the most important and respected positions. Water, like food and air, is essential for survival.

Corporations and colleges and hospitals can become sustaining institutions like tribes. They can be the source of belonging; they can be the locus for achievement; they can be a real life- and work-support system. The best institutions have already become these things.

This is not to say that a company or an institu- tion has to be one big happy family. If it is, some- thing is probably wrong. Diversity of opinion is as necessary as light and air, a diversity of opinion encouraged and exploited for the good of the group. Leaders help define that public good; the watercarriers of an institution communicate and exemplify the ties that bind the institution to- gether.

What does it mean to be a watercarrier in a modern-day corporation or institution? What are the essentials that corporate watercarriers bring to organizations?

Before we had a third shift at Herman Miller, we had a rather primitive system of alerting main- tenance people to problems when the plant was empty. One element of this system allowed the telephone to ring in Gord Nagelkirk's home if the water pressure at the plant dropped. This way Gord would know if a sprinkler went off, indicating a fire.

Gord lived about eight miles from the plant in a small village, where, in fact, he was on a party line. Any nocturnal call on our alarm system would also waken several other people in the town. One night at 2 A.M., our makeshift alarm went off. Gord got dressed immediately, drove his pickup truck to the plant, and began to walk carefully through all of the buildings. Many of you will know that walking through a dark factory at night can be a disconcerting experience. Even walking through a forest at night is more predictable.

After a thorough check, he was able to find no problem, but since the water pressure gauge continued to indicate an abnormality, Gord could not let the matter rest. He rechecked the entire interior of each of the buildings. Still he found nothing. Then he decided to walk around the outside of each building to make sure that no water was escaping there. Again he found nothing.

At that time we had just completed a new building, not yet in use, and Gord couldn't imagine a problem there. Nevertheless, he decided to check it. Halfway around the exterior of the new building, he sank up to his knees in mud. He discovered that a six-inch water line under the foundation had broken. Had he not been persistent, the entire north wall of the building would have collapsed by morning.

I have often asked myself what it was that made Gord so persistent. At that moment in the middle of the night, Gord felt that the consequences of his behavior were personal. His commitment to the company extended and strengthened the quality of an entire organization.

People like Gord bring to mind words such as vitality and renewal and life-giving. To be a watercarrier (though Gord, of course, had to stop the water!) suggests continuity, longevity, com-

mitment, dependability, and resourcefulness.
Watercarriers transfer the essence of the institution to new people who arrive to help us and,
eventually, to replace us. They understand that
resources can be nourished as well as managed.
All of the visions, all of the strategies, all of the
implementation, all of the day-to-day operations,
are carried out by one potential watercarrier or
another, always working in concert with, and in
need of, other potential watercarriers.

What is it that transforms potential watercarriers into actual ones? I'm not sure I know the
answer. Some people become watercarriers in six
months. Some never do. When I think of the
watercarriers I know, I think of qualities like compassion, humor, a sense of history, the ability to
teach, and an unshakable commitment to the
tribe.

Lyndon Johnson once said that we need people
"more concerned with the quality of their goals
than the quantity of their goods." Watercarriers
help determine and then perpetuate the quality of

an institution's goals. They bring the unity of the tribe to organizations, the confident and relaxed unity of a group of people dedicated to a common goal and bound together by a covenant. The covenant expresses the beliefs held in common, the values shared, the goals and ideas and ideals to which everyone has made a common commitment.

Watercarriers help us see beyond the ephemeral.

I like to think about management in two broad categories, scientific and tribal. The tribal is certainly the most important and, while palpable, is quite difficult to grasp and nurture. Tribal implies membership, and it implies territorial or functional accountabilities. Tribal carries connotations of social and corporate structure, including clans and age grades, and it can illuminate for us meaningful connections to our ancestors and elders.

Tribal also means shared goals but different and separate responsibilities. No organization, even a tribe, can survive without diversity of opinion, approach and responsibility. Corporate life is just too complex. If I knew everything about the organization I work for, I would probably be familiar with nothing. Intimacy with one's own job requires you to remain ignorant about some things, to trust to others, to be thankful that other people know more than you do! In that way, a tribe survives. Organizations grow under pressure, when a change or a crisis reveals new strengths from all quarters.

You can't be hired into a tribe. Joining a tribe results from, and results in, a certain intimacy. This intimacy links the talents and skills that each of us brings to the job and the corporation on behalf of our customers—with marvelously delightful and worthwhile results. Intimacy springs from relationships rigorous, disciplined, and with many constraints. There are failures as well as successes.

At some companies, people come to understand that corporate tribalism lies at the heart of

why so many people from such a variety of cultures make over the years such unusual contributions to corporate life. Those people realize the
value of tribal storytellers, the custodians of the
history and values and culture of the group. Any
healthy organization, like a good tribe, needs certain rituals and symbols like company picnics,
outstanding employee awards, and memorial
works of art. Watercarriers revel in such things.

Watercarriers thrive in diversity and understand the fragility of organizations. People, relationships, values, and beliefs are most important
to a corporation and, fittingly, the most fragile
components. Watercarriers comprehend and pre-
serve them. That's why I have included this essay
in my book.

At Herman Miller, many watercarriers have
served our company over the years and still serve
there. These are the people who, like many in all
organizations, have invested their lives in a significant way in the corporation. The following is a
list of things important to watercarriers at Her-

man Miller. Do you have a list for your organization?

What's important and why we are what we are—our history.

The fragile aspects of our future.

Relationships. They rest on what counts and what's right, on who counts and who's right. What counts are the things we believe, our understanding of people, and our embracing of diversity.

Our commitment to problem-solving and good design, a passion for the way in which things ought to be done.

Our beliefs and goals, our inheritance when we arrived in this corporation—the most important things we can leave behind, our legacy to our corporate heirs.

The need for continuity and reliability in the leaders of our company.

The essential role played by longtime followers in the life of the organization. Only followers can give an organization this.

Change. Change without continuity is chaos. Continuity without change is sloth—and very risky.

The provision of necessities and the bearing of standards. This duty lies not solely with management.

Before I stepped down as CEO, I searched around for a way to honor the watercarriers whom I had known and the ones who would come after me. I discovered a sculpture in Arizona by Allan Houser. An American Indian, he knew all about watercarriers. His own culture honors them. The result of his talent is a wonderful and evocative sculpture titled *Watercarrier*. Around it on a low granite plinth at the company headquarters are the names of people who have served Herman Miller for twenty years or more, an investment of their lives that has contributed to the continuity of our company. Every year, of course, we add new names. I'm impressed by the number of people devoting this much energy to a single organization.

To dedicate the sculpture and its lovely setting, we invited all the people to the ceremony whose names would be placed on the granite plinth. Their presence at the dedication made it a memorable day. It occurred to me that these people, though many had retired from the company, had come back to create a new part of its history.

A small version of Houser's sculpture sits outside the CEO's office to make sure that Herman Miller's leaders don't forget the importance of continuity and history in the rush of everyday business. History can't be left to fend for itself. For when it comes to history and beliefs and values, we turn our future on the lathe of the past.

Ropes or
Bathrooms
.....

Late one night in 1969, David Williams and I were scouring the city of Bath, England, for a hotel room. We had been looking for a place to establish a new company to manufacture office furniture in England. So far, we were the only two employees. Perhaps that was why we had failed to reserve a room at a hotel.

Finally after eleven o'clock, we went into the lobby of an old, four-story wooden pension with a lighted front porch. David walked up to the man at the desk and asked for two rooms. "I have one with a bath and one with a rope," he said. "Good, we'll take them," David said. A true Englishman to his marrow, David continued. "He's American," he said, pointing at me, "give him the bath. I'll take the rope."

I was tired and didn't think much about it until I started to unpack in my room on the top floor of the old hotel. I *did* have a room with a bath. Then I got to wondering what David had. Too curious to go to sleep, I walked down the hall to David's room. "Since I have the room with the bath, what in the world do you have?" I asked him through the door. He took me into the room, and there on the floor next to the window was a coil of rope with one end tied to a cast-iron radiator. "In these old buildings," David said, "you've got to have a fire escape."

In retrospect, that experience seems to me to be an interesting emblem of an aspect of democratic capitalism, a system that always boils down to a series of choices like the one David faced that night in Bath. It's a system of free choices, each one laden with consequences. Freedom, choices, and consequences are inherent in the system. I happen to think that the greatness of the system results from these three characteristics—enormous freedom, clear choices, and inevitable consequences. The key to succeeding in the system lies in the way we exploit our freedom, make our choices, and anticipate the consequences.

It's deceptively simple. I would like to examine some freedoms, some choices, and some consequences that seem to me, at least, to be of particular significance if we are to discover new horizons in democratic capitalism.

People who spent time in the Communist-dominated Eastern European countries saw first-

hand the staleness and the boredom and the inef-
fectiveness that blossom in a society without the
freedom to choose. (And now, of course, that is
changing.) At the same time, that experience
makes clear anew what a marvelous and fundamental right we have in the freedom to choose. In
a sense, the freedom to choose is uniquely a capitalist's privilege and a capitalist's burden. People
without choices don't have to worry much about
it. People with the freedom to choose have to
consider their choices, and the act of choosing, of
course, has a catch—the consequences.

As a way of thinking about this matter, I'll
touch briefly on five subjects about which people
in corporate and institutional settings make
choices all the time: the customer (or the student
or the patient); the role of change; accountability,
both personal and corporate; beauty and harmony; and the quality of our relationships.

The customer. In our system, the one indispensable ingredient is the customer. In dealing with

customers, when we choose a way to behave, we are forced to face up to the consequences. You don't need me to describe to you the vicissitudes of air travel in the United States. In contrast, it's interesting to listen to people who travel frequently to Asia. They talk at length about the quality of service they receive in the hotels of Hong Kong and Singapore. In the matter of serving customers, the difference between a Hong Kong hotel and an airline in the United States is something about which we need to think seriously. The difference is not one of skill or education or experience. It's a matter of values. To be customer-oriented is not to be self-oriented.

(In all fairness, I don't want to overlook the delightfully disorienting smell of chocolate chip cookies baking in the galleys of Midwest Express's airplanes.)

Hotels in Hong Kong and airlines in the United States have made a choice. They and their customers must live with the consequences.

The role of change. Change and all its ramifications dominate the conversations and preoccupy the thinking of organizational people. For many years, my father-in-law was confined to a nursing home, having been seriously paralyzed by a stroke. His mind clear and active, he observed keenly much that went on among the other residents.

The management of the home had a problem. Two older gentlemen, not as clear of mind as my father-in-law, made a habit of escaping together. The nurses were justifiably anxious, for these two residents were liable to all kinds of dangers out in the hustle and bustle of the traffic and the community. Something had to change.

One day the manager of the nursing home confided to my father-in-law that he was at his wits' end. What could he do about these two old friends? Obviously they could not be restrained in their rooms, but neither could they be allowed to endanger themselves outside the nursing home. My father-in-law's suggestion was a great expression of voice and touch. He said, "These two men have lived a long time, and their habits are not going to change. All of their lives, they have put on their hats when they go outside. I'm sure that if you hide their hats, they'll no longer try to escape." And sure enough, that solved the problem. Of course, there are many other kinds of change.

- Technological change opens new horizons and requires new learning and new skills. More often than not, technological change leads to corporate renewal.

- Competitive change is one of the secrets of effective businesses, churches, and schools. It keeps us alert. If we pay attention, it helps us to survive. It surely ought to keep us humble. Competitive change can be an unloving, but nearly always helpful, confrontation —a splash of cold water on those mornings of our complacency.

- International change is relatively new in the lives of North Americans. Global competition is revealing to us novel work codes, new concepts of service, and levels of quality different from what we have thought necessary. Some European universities have been trying to adjust for quite a few years to that very kind of competition from universities in the United States.

· Social change never stops. Perhaps never before has a society changed as much as ours has since the late 1950s. We find ourselves with a few advances and not a little uncertainty. The advent of more equity for minorities, the increasing number of women in the workplace, and the rearrangement of our concept of the family are kinds of changes we deal with daily.

We are not free to choose to avoid dealing with change. The only thing to decide is how to deal with change once you create it yourself or once you find it staring you in the face. I believe two attitudes will guide us into constructive responses to change.

First, it's important to understand that neither change nor the person who leads us to change is our enemy. I have heard leaders described as people who ask their institutions to change. Certainly Abraham Lincoln became a leader not by justifying the beliefs of a large number of his constituents, but by changing those beliefs.

If we could persuade first graders that change is not an enemy, our lives as parents would be easier. If faculties and universities could accept change as simply a chance for good or ill, the learning process would be far less autocratic and far more effective. If folks in business and industry could accept that, we would be more competitive. Beware of people who make of change a cause of failure.

Second, the rate of change today requires that each of us become a frantic learner. Otherwise, change will leave us as forgotten in the past as the people who predicted the failure of the automobile. If learning, by itself, were not such a wonderful process, we might have reason to complain. But learning is worthwhile and meaningful in and of itself. Leaders respond to change by learning something. The eager, frantic learners in life find actual joy in the process of change.

Dr. Mitchell Rabkin, CEO of Beth Israel Hospital in Boston, keeps on his desk a small sculpture of a boy squatted on his haunches in that position we all recognize, picking up something and looking it over. The statue is there, he says, to remind him just how important curiosity and endless learning are to everybody.

The freedom to choose to be personally and, therefore, institutionally, accountable. Naturally this entails asking "Accountable for what?" and "To whom?" These are precisely the kinds of questions that so many boards of directors and boards of trustees should be asking themselves. I imagine that quite a few stockholders and faculty members and students would like to hear the answers.

I'll ask you to consider the following elements of personal accountability.

- Quality: Quality of life, quality of neighborhood, quality of product. Here are some reasonable questions about quality: What am I going to choose when I think about quality? Do I think about it in the first place? Is it important? Is it related to truth, awareness, and joy in my life? Does my leader think about quality? How does my leader speak of quality to the organization? Does the president of the company give the same attention to the grounds around the factory as to the lawn around her home?

- Service: What does the word service really mean? (Service is an idea that really defies words.) How am I personally going to be accountable for service? Am I going to practice what I observe on domestic airlines? Or am I going to practice what I learn about service in Hong Kong hotels?

- Choosing what to measure: Surely everybody knows how to measure results. We grade students, tally up sales, and time the hundred-meter dash. We work hard to stay within a budget. We know we have to make a profit—financial or otherwise—because it's one of the costs of the future. But leaders need to choose what to measure in life. The real booby trap is to measure the wrong things. Good short-term results are not synonymous with long-term needs; good numbers don't result from managing numbers.

- Grace: You may be puzzled as to how to deal with this. Each time I raise this issue with people in small groups, they ask me what the word grace means. Well, grace happens to be an interesting word. Almost any dictionary will offer you several inches of explanation for the word, covering everything from good manners to aesthetic qualities to theological concepts. With a word like grace, you must choose a definition—another choice!

Grace is a lot like a work of modern art. You can add your own perspective, your own interpretation, your own experience. Often you may take more away from a painting than the artist put into it. I also think of grace in the corporate world as an unearned and unearnable right.

Ask this question about your institution: What can grace enable us to be? Think of it as a choice.

Beauty and harmony. Leaders make choices about beauty and harmony all the time. I'd like to ask, in your corporation or institution or your family, do you choose to care about beauty and harmony? For people who do, it's always an uphill battle. It always will be.

Everyone needs to see beauty and harmony as a choice, something to be accountable for. In the United States, the process of taking great chunks of our country and turning them into strip malls and parking lots has become a specialty for too many people. In some grand old neighborhoods, it may take a couple of generations for this to happen. In other instances, cabals of hard-driving capitalists and elected officials are experts in the fine art of making it happen overnight.

Many people spend a third of their lives working in buildings without windows. Blacktop covers good earth. Noble old trees lose their hearts to make room for power lines. The exercise of capitalist license has produced unbelievable consequences for all of us. Where are the chief executive officers or chief financial officers who read Thoreau's *Walden* or Rachel Carson's *Silent Spring?* Where are the business schools and engineering schools that require students to read Peter Blake's *God's Own Junkyard* or George Nelson's *How to See?* Is it really the case that the capitalist system will always be visually illiterate?

I don't happen to believe that we must capitulate to ugliness and dissonance. We don't have to connect every decision about our environment or product design or trees or signage solely to first costs or return on assets or the eternal shortage of parking. Achieving a prescribed return on assets is not part of the law of the Medes and Persians, you know. It's only one of a long list of items for which we are accountable. Decisions on the beauty and harmony of an environment are not the province of the financial department or the developer or even the person who owns the land. These decisions are the proper concern of an enormous public, since no one can walk through the results of such decisions without encountering the consequences. Once a building is up or a tree is grown, it belongs to all of us. And it either blesses or embarrasses us.

If we do choose beauty and harmony, we give ourselves a unique, competitive advantage. Universities and colleges with beautiful campuses do have a leg up in the competition for the best students. Stores that choose beauty and harmony do have an advantage. Organizations that steadfastly pursue beauty and harmony do attract the best people. Not to choose beauty and harmony puts one squarely in the ranks of the mediocre and endows one with all the characteristics that word implies.

We must understand a fundamental and dangerous consequence: Once taken, the path toward beauty and harmony will not allow any member of an organization to stray. Beauty and harmony must become a red thread through an organization and all that it does—products, services, communications, plant layout and sales strategy, architecture and facility management. Beauty and harmony must surface in our relationships as well as in our architecture.

There's one important thing to understand about beauty and harmony—it's a universal, not an elitist, choice.

Relationships. What kind of choices will we make in the future about ourselves? In our families and in our corporations and in our institutions, we are able to choose the basis on which we will work with each other. We do get to choose whether in our hearts we will respect and build on our diversity or ignore it. We can choose to be hospitable to unusual persons and ideas or we can shun them. We can choose, each of us, to accept the authenticity of every person in an organization or to deny people the chance to be included.

You see, all these choices have to do with a larger question: Are we ready to trust each other and to give each other the space to reach our potential? The entire well-being of a family or an institution or a corporation depends on a confident answer of "Yes, we are ready to help each other reach our personal potential."

Reaching goals is fine for an annual plan. Only reaching one's potential is fine for a life.

Our choices in all these areas—and many others—come ready-made with consequences. The consequences depend on all kinds of things: the nature of the organization; the poetry of its leaders; the strength of its relationships. People who stand up and make these choices (for without action, your choice will be made for you) are like parents with teenage children—you can't know

everything, but you do get to live with the consequences! We really wouldn't want it any other
way.

The real danger lies in blind complacency. Not
to see our choices may be worse than making poor
decisions. Be alive to the alternatives. What will
it be for you? The rope or the bath?

Leaders'
Leaders

.....

The relatively short history of the United States glistens with innovations. Our open, democratic meritocracy has bred and nurtured unusual persons with unusual ideas.

Innovation is a form of change. For

the most part, our culture welcomes change, although more discernment would no doubt be welcome. We do run into, as you might expect, barriers to change: Grandchildren do tend to get around more easily than grandparents. As our society becomes more complex, we find important segments of it becoming larger, more structured, more bureaucratic, less nimble, less open, and less hospitable to unusual persons. Leaders can, however, resist hardening of the arteries.

To some kinds of problems we can apply known and tested formulas with good results. But with more serious societal and competitive problems, we need to reach somehow for the renewal and innovation and vitality required for truly lasting solutions.

I happen to believe that a large part of the secret lies in how individual leaders in a great variety of settings make room for people who have unusual and creative gifts and temporarily become followers themselves.

Leaders' leaders stand out from the rest of us.

Somehow their contributions affect large groups and move organizations toward something better; yet they function, for the most part, outside of organizations. The changes they bring are more like leaps than the small steps most of us use. They think of the world in large terms—they work for institutions or societies or cultures, not for individuals. Leaders work to bring the special and creative gifts of these people to bear on the efforts of the group.

We may not find overall solutions to society's needs on a grand scale. National leaders and CEOs of big corporations cannot be counted on to do the good work for all leaders. Hundreds of leaders in companies and colleges and banks, in churches and government, in high schools and museums, already have chosen to follow the gifted people who can bring renewal, vitality, and opportunity.

Once a leader decides to accept this kind of responsibility, we can define the process quickly.

I would call it a search for beneficial surprise.

Traditional education does not prepare us for this. We must search for a creative fecundity, a compost heap of experience and ideas, experiments and failures and successes, that will bring about the changes and improvements we need.

If we are to find new sources and perspectives, it seems to me that there are at least three areas of special concern, which, if thoughtfully considered, are likely to yield good results.

1. How does a leader approach the process of creative work? A leader first makes a personal commitment to be hospitable to gifted people, a broad commitment to open herself to contributions from many quarters. At some time or other, many people from the working population contribute in special situations and special settings in a creative way. A leader makes her commitment to all.

The commitment entails a number of ideas and guidelines. Let me give you some starters.

A leader protects unusual persons from the bureaucracy and legalism so ensconced in our organizations.

A leader remains vulnerable to real surprise and to true quality. I do mean surprise—something totally unexpected. I also mean a new level of quality, one that I might not have considered before. Neither of these things is easy; really great ideas shake up organizations.

A leader works with creative people without fear. A wise counselor to Herman Miller once advised a key executive to get to know one of the truly creative designers who have worked with our company. The executive, perhaps a little uncomfortable with the prospect of meeting face-to-face and alone with the designer, failed to heed the advice. When the counselor asked about the visit, the executive responded by saying that he knew it would do him good to set up the meeting. The counselor replied, "I'm not worried about what *you're* missing. The *company* needs you to know this person."

While respecting them, a leader is wary of incremental changes. Don't let small changes—perfectly good in their own right—replace true creativity and real innovation.

A leader does not demand unreasonable personal or corporate loyalty. She should realize that creative people are loyal to the idea (or, for instance, the movement) and appear to others to be nonjoiners. I realize that this is difficult. Creative people need breadth and the assurance of fair treatment rather than isolation and control.

A leader arranges for projects to proceed along a narrowing path. The majority of data and opinions, dreams and constraints, should be made available at the beginning. Necessary disciplines and involved departments must all be heard from in the formative stages. Then a leader will narrow involvements and focus responsibilities and begin a careful—but not oppressive—scrutiny of progress and direction. Only a few people can take the risk and have the real competence required to finish the job.

In the end, true innovation will never be a democratic event—it's just too risky for groupthink. Majorities seldom vote to change. A small group of accountable leaders together with the creative people involved must make the decision and take the risk. If you're fortunate enough to come across a truly revolutionary idea, remember what Peter Drucker once said: "When you have a real innovation, don't compromise."

A leader paves the way for change. She prepares the organization. Probably the most important preparation is lavish communication. We can neither read each other's minds nor afford the sin of isolation. Yet each of us needs to be able to identify with a mission. Each person needs to decide to follow: When you ask someone to do something, make sure you wait for an answer.

At Herman Miller when I was CEO and reporting monthly to all of the Scanlon work team leaders, we would distribute some of my comments at the monthly performance review sessions to as many people as wished to read them. It was a good way to keep people informed and involved.

One day my secretary received a call from Bill Manifold, a young purchasing agent, asking for an appointment. Bill arrived in my office on the date we had set. In his hands were copies of three of my speeches; each speech had paragraphs underlined with green felt-tip pen.

Bill proceeded to fire detailed questions at me, some aimed at helping him understand my ideas a little better, but some demonstrating to me that I was not communicating very well. The session turned into an interesting and educational experience for both of us, and other such sessions followed. Bill taught me how to sharpen my ability to communicate persistently within a participative framework. I learned that if you're a leader and you're not sick and tired of communicating, you probably aren't doing a good enough job.

A leader sets the example for openness and imagination and acceptance. A leader shows by example how to live constructively with eccentricity. She understands that creative people can be the most effective teachers in an organization, and she will prepare the classroom.

In selecting architects for building projects over a number of years at Herman Miller, one of the key questions we asked ourselves was "Who among these very good architects will teach us the most?"

A leader knows that the organization must understand how important it is to have a chance to meet unmet needs. Creative people thrive on research, intuition, and their own perceptions; unswerving faith in conventional wisdom frustrates them. They need large doses of diverse experience, because their work is often a process of discovering and connecting.

The organization must also understand that creative people are inwardly compelled to do their work. As with amateurs (see "Amateurs"), the usual corporate incentives may not motivate creative people. A writer, when asked why he wrote, replied, "Because I have to, not because I like to."

Creative people have to be involved; they have to make a difference. They may trouble smooth operations, but at the same time they have a gift for capitalizing on constraints.

2. What do creative people need to be fruitful in the worlds of organizations?

First, they need access to (even intimacy with) senior leadership. A leader will let it be known that this relationship is important, that creative people on the team do not contribute from the fringes.

Creative work needs the ethos of jazz. I've already mentioned the lessons to be learned from a jazz band. A leader will pick the tune, set the tempo, and start the music, define a "style." After that, it's up to the band to be disciplined and free, wild and restrained—leaders and followers, focused and wide-ranging, playing the music for the audi-

Leaders' Leaders
· · · · ·

ence and accountable to the requirements of the band. Jazz-band leaders know how to integrate the "voices" in the band without diminishing their uniqueness. The individuals in the band are expected to play solo and together. What a wonderful way to think of a vital and productive organization!

It matters a great deal *how* leaders give work to gifted followers. In 1977, Herman Miller built a manufacturing building in Bath, England, which won the *Financial Times* award as the best industrial building of the year. Nicholas Grimshaw, the architect, said at the time that the quality of the building could never have been achieved without the poetry and requirements of the brief given to him by Herman Miller. (I've discussed the essence of this brief in *Leadership Is an Art*.)

Creative people, like the rest of us, need constraints. Like facts, constraints become the friends of the people I'm talking about. One of the most striking characteristics of the creative people I know is their ability to renew themselves through constraints.

A *leader needs to give creative people license to be contrary*. Leaders will use wisely the essential contribution made through contrary opinion. Cynicism has no place in an organization and the relationships with its institutional publics, but leaders welcome the committed skeptic, who wants to be held accountable and demands a share of the risk.

Leaders give odds to creative people that their work will get to market. Whatever the results are—a product or service, information or communication —there must be the potential of reality lying ahead as creative people meander along toward real innovation. They need to know that they will have help in making the results of their work real.

Creative people need a fundamental level of trust from leaders. True leaders will not hover over every detail but will leave that to the person entrusted with the project. Industrial designer Bill

Stumpf, one of the most creative people I know, wrote me that a leader's expression of trust creates the grace necessary for creative people to operate.

The work of creative people is only part of a whole; it cannot be taken in isolation. Again Bill Stumpf: When a company works with a designer, it works with "a designer in total—his theories, philosophy, reputation, and talent. In a sense the product is a part of a larger whole."

Finally, creative people need to work with others of equal competence. Tennis can be played at many levels of ability. We improve only when we are challenged and stretched. This is also the way it is at work. Things surely go better when we're paired with real competence.

3. What should a leader be careful about when dealing with creative people?

First, a leader will be careful about the utilitarian self-concept so much in favor with administrators. Return on assets has become a Baal in too many organiza-

tions. All things cannot, and must not, be quanti-
fied. Financial and legal matters are truly important, but they do not lie at the heart of our future.
Resist the urge to structure all things alike.

*Second, just as moving up in the hierarchy does not
confer competence, so organizational power does not
guarantee wisdom.* The discernment and judgment
necessary to evaluate creative gifts and true innovation, to doom or give life to good design or
engineering breakthroughs, lie in the province of
people trained in those fields. Leaders owe it to
themselves and their organizations to delegate
such judgments to people more qualified than
they.

Be careful about what you nurture. The perfect lab-
oratory or the finest research facility can be very
seductive. Leaders are understandably tempted to
focus on the context. But a leader's true love
should be the people who do the work. She
should nurture her relationships with those per-

sons. As a physician once remarked to me, "You can't learn surgery in a comfortable office."

Be wary of setting out to win prizes. Truly creative people flourish in the process of solving problems. Good work is the goal; recognition is a consequence.

A last caution: Don't fail to give credit. People who through their unusual gifts bring change and innovation and renewal to organizations need to be identified. Organizations need to know the sources of their vitality; leaders acknowledge these sources with fidelity. A friend of mine noticed buried among the stems in an arrangement of flowers a small tag that said "Created by number 59." This does not qualify as credit; creativity does not proceed from anonymous sources.

Both personally and organizationally, the results of becoming a good leader for creative people are surely worth the effort. Leaders may expect a legacy going beyond quarterly results. They may expect products and services that deliver a truly competitive edge. There will be beneficial surprises, not predictable solutions or designs by committee. Change and renewal and hope and confidence will result. There will be a higher level of civility and robust institutional health. Making the effort to be a leader to creative people and learning to follow them signal both real leadership competence and the understanding that such work comes from the heart and not from a management handbook.

In leading people who bring the gift of creativity to organizations, as in leading anyone, leaders will have to examine their deepest, most heartfelt beliefs—and act on them.

Take Five

· · · · ·

Fernando de Padova, our handsome and urbane Italian business partner, was on his first business trip to Denmark. He had been traveling for a long time to get to Copenhagen, and he sat down with great anticipation to dinner. The waiter in the elegant restaurant Fernando had chosen brought the menu, and he was faced with a great choice of food.

He told me later that he was too vain to admit to a waiter in a hotel that he couldn't read Danish. But Fernando studied the menu for a time and called the waiter back to the table. Pointing with a flourish to an item on the menu, he ordered his dinner. The waiter nodded, left the table, and came back soon with an enormous plate of olives.

Though Fernando had failed only in ordering dinner, consider what would happen if his attitude had prevailed at a board meeting or in Congress or in a college president's office. I have come to realize that I have depended on followers for many things—spirit, commitment, inspiration, expertise. They are the ones who make a vision real, and at the very heart of leadership lies the necessity of making it possible for followers to contribute. Followers need a chance to do their best; leaders need a lot of help.

If through voice and touch one can create a field that lies open to all, the furrows will be plowed. And then falls to leaders perhaps the most rewarding part of their jobs—acknowledging the efforts of other people and saying thank you.

You can tell by now that a book like this has many roots. It has grown over the course of many years, tended carefully—though in many cases unwittingly—by a large family. Ruth, for instance, and Zoe, and many people with whom I've worked closely over the years in a variety of settings have all helped me in one way or other become a better leader and have thus played a part in this book. Some—Carla, Egbert, Ed, Carol, Manuel—appear in various chapters. Some people, too many to name here, have helped me to understand late in life the essential nature of the marriage of competence and morality, the connection between beliefs and behavior, the weaving of voice and touch.

As the chapter before explained, leaders find many teachers and enablers. The lore of life, the way to one's voice, comes more from mistakes than achievements, more from listening than talking, more from these teachers and enablers than from one's own understanding. Working as a trustee for twenty-five years with the community of people at Fuller Theological Seminary has helped me find my voice. As in many other areas of my life, people who care for me have helped me. And without them, most of my dreams would still be visions. This book is no exception.

Every manuscript needs its true critics, serious friends who contribute objectivity and fresh perspectives. They made the comments and asked the questions that enabled me to rethink, revise, and polish. Such friends are Jim O'Toole and Lew Smedes, David Hubbard and Bill Stumpf, Luanne Selk and Matti Lainema, Michele Hunt and Steve Frykholm. With counselors like these, one always expects the melody to pass from player to player.

And where would I be without my family to

keep an eye on me? (I can hear the answers to that question now!) My wife, Esther, and most of my children have also read the manuscript for *Leadership Jazz* and have given good advice.

One consistent piece of advice given to authors (and this goes for leaders, too, for writing a book is remarkably like many of the projects leaders face) is to get a good editor. I have done exactly that. I got a great one, Clark Malcolm. As we worked together on this book and *Leadership Is an Art*, he's become more than an editor. He has also been a conscience, mentor, devil's advocate, and caring friend. We've become so close that we sometimes joke about whose words are whose. Clark has been college teacher and carpenter. He has intimated to me the value of fishing, plays classical music on the piano, and tells me stories about shooting mistletoe out of oak trees in Arkansas, where he grew up. Leaders often run across people like Clark.

The relationships I have with all of these people are central to my ability to write this book, because each of these people is a living expression of the message in *Leadership Jazz*.

You're probably now halfway through this book. If you've been reading and reflecting and making connections in your own mind, and if you've begun to scribble between the lines and in the margins—if you've begun to fill up the figurative and literal space in *Leadership Jazz*—you, too, have become part of the fabric of this book and the ideas in it. And you have joined the group of people to whom I want to say thank you.

Have you taken five to ponder the nature of the contribution that other people make to your leadership? I highly recommend it.

What Would Bucky Say?

· · · · ·

Charles Eames, looked on by many as the foremost furniture designer of the twentieth century, has influenced my professional life for a long time. He designed our family home in 1954. Even these many years after his death in 1978, his way of thinking still occurs to me.

As a designer of furniture, exhibits, and graphics, he was one of Herman Miller's most significant teachers and leaders during the corporation's formative years. By the time he died, Charles had also become an extraordinary filmmaker. He combined beautiful talent, intimacy with both the problem and the customer, enormous commitment, and great insight into the role of constraints. He blessed the lives of many thousands of people with unparalleled quality and joy and improved every area in which he worked.

In Charles's sometimes single-minded pursuit of quality and goodness and worth, he constantly measured what he did against a high standard, one that he set for himself. In the process of measuring himself and his work, he faced the same problem that you and I face. Leaders are constantly called upon to measure something—performance, the value of an asset, the potential of a vice president. But how are leaders to measure their own performance? Since the effects of a leader's decisions and actions are often not apparent until months, sometimes years later, measuring a leader's contribution is especially difficult.

Nevertheless, leaders need some way to gauge how they're doing, whether they are helping the organization or hurting it. Like every member of a group, a leader is, after all, accountable for her performance.

The solution for me naturally rises out of the questions leaders ask. The quality of our work as leaders and the quality of our lives depends significantly on the questions we ask and the people about whom we ask the questions.

The company I work for, Herman Miller, always seems to be more comfortable operating our manufacturing plants in small towns than in big cities. I once asked Eames, "What is it that makes small towns special? How are we going to distinguish the elements of small towns that are important to a company that has quality as one of its chief goals?" Charles suggested that I ask two questions about a prospective community: "What is the quality of their bread?" and "What is the quality of their parades?"

In Eames's case, he had many people to whom he could address his questions. But the key question he asked himself consistently was "What would Bucky say?" Buckminster Fuller, as I guess you can figure out, was a touchstone for all that mattered to Charles.

Buckminster Fuller is a difficult man to label. He was thinker, architect, sociologist, engineer, poet, inventor of the geodesic dome—he was a gifted and perceptive person. Secretary-General of the United Nations U Thant called him "one of the greatest philosopher-scientists of our time." By choosing Bucky as the ultimate judge, Charles certainly set his standards high.

As I worked on this book I asked myself, "What would Charles and Lew Smedes and David Hubbard say?" Then I'm afraid I took the added precaution of asking Lew and David themselves!

I'm sure you already have a set of questions you

ask yourself about leadership, depending on your discipline or industry or institution. Let me suggest some more as a way of measuring our progress toward becoming better leaders. Perhaps you haven't thought of these, and I hope you will add to this list. Together we can make some headway.

- When was the last time I called to say thank you?

- How long ago was it that I actually saw the products my business sells being made? A college president might ask, how long ago has it been since I visited a classroom? Or taught a class?

- How often do I say "I don't know"? When I left Basel, Switzerland, to return to the United States after working there for some time, my Swiss co-workers gave me a fireman's hat with the following message written in the local Swiss dialect: "I don't know for sure." They apparently thought it unusual to have an American manager who admitted that he didn't know everything. I still try to remember how much there is that I don't know.

- When did I last call a customer and ask how we're doing?

- Do faculty want me to share in their departmental celebrations?

- Am I inadvertently bruising the spirit or obstructing the performance of the people for whom I am responsible?

- Who matters?

- What effect does time have on what I measure? Is what I measure today different from what I would measure when I'm seventy? Would the light of mortality affect my vision?

- Has anyone in this place confided in me lately?

- Are followers becoming restless, tentative, or uncertain?

- Do I have a nose for stale air? Have things become mechanical? Conservative? Do people here avoid risk like the plague and isolate themselves? Do some folks here fear a dreadful fading of the dream and see only visions of greed and power and a petty, capricious value system?

- Have we stopped hiring people better than we are?

- What is truth? Is it quality? Is it a person? Or is it a concept? Does it encompass patience and grace?

- Have I learned to stop? Do I stop to talk or listen, or simply out of curiosity?

- What matters?

- When did I last spend three full hours with someone from research and development? (You might look at "Leaders' Leaders" for more about this.)

- Do I realize that special insight often comes out of silence? Do I practice "systematic neglect"? Robert Greenleaf discusses these two intriguing ideas in his wonderful parable *Teacher as Servant*.

- When did I last abandon a program?

- Followers sometimes treat leaders like an emperor. Do I have my clothes on? Do people tell me when I'm naked?

- Is the organization I work for getting to be more like a symphony by Beethoven? Why isn't a college like a symphony by Beethoven? Why can't institutions encompass comfortably and constructively the normal range of human emotions and aspirations and triumphs and failures?

- Have I made it possible for the institution to succeed after I leave?

- Is the organization succeeding at the expense of individual potential? It is the leader's special province to guard the chance of individuals to reach their potential. Have I checked lately to see that this opportunity exists and that people know I care about it?

· Am I willing to let others see how I wish to be measured?

Bill Caudill, the fine architect, teacher, and author, served for many years on the Herman Miller board of directors. In that role, Bill made a unique and priceless contribution. Selecting Bill for our board was, as it is for every member, a very serious matter. We work from a written statement of criteria for board membership, and we seek a diverse group of members so that the diverse needs of the corporation can be met. When I went to Houston to ask Bill whether he might consider serving on the board, he was immediately interested. An architect, Bill was well aware of Herman Miller's reputation, but he wasn't going to consent immediately. He had some questions of his own he wanted to answer.

He wanted to visit Zeeland, Michigan, the

community that hosts our corporate headquarters and main manufacturing site. And on the appointed day of his visit, he walked into my office midmorning, shook my hand, and said that yes, he would serve on Herman Miller's board of directors.

You can imagine my curiosity about how he had arrived at his decision. I asked if he would like to discuss anything further. He told me that he had found out everything he needed to know that morning at Bosch's restaurant in Zeeland, one of those typical Midwestern, small-town institutions where local folks gather to sort out hometown matters and world affairs. Bill had joined one of the groups he found at a large table and had quizzed them about Herman Miller and its standing in the community. He told them that he was being considered for a position on Herman Miller's board of directors. What did they think of that? After talking to Bill, understanding who he was, and answering his questions, together they agreed that Bill should accept the position.

Then he had driven to the local cemetery to make sure that only live plants and fresh flowers were allowed on the graves. He said, "I couldn't work in a town where they use plastic flowers."

Such were the kinds of questions a bona fide leader asked himself.

Where Do Ethics and Leadership Intersect?

.....

Believe me, they do intersect, all the time. This seems to surprise people in business. I read more and more about ethics and business, courses in business schools, and consultants in ethics, as if the corporate world had finally discov-

ered ethics. Of course, this isn't true. Relationships in business, like any relationships, need to
stand up to ethical scrutiny. When do the ethical
beliefs of a leader cross her commitments to an
organization? When should a leader's judgments
of right and wrong, of good and bad, impinge on
the group of followers?

Other people have written entire books about
ethics and business. Not having the qualifications
for that, I would simply like to explore ways of
reflecting on the interplay of ethics and leadership. One of the ways I deal with this is to remind
myself of the question: "To whom do I answer?"

One of the most sacred relationships among
teams of people is that between leaders and followers. This relationship, so central and crucial,
depends to an extraordinary degree on the clearly
expressed and consistently demonstrated values of
the leader as seen through the special lens of followers. This is why leadership and ethics are inex-
tricably woven together.

As my world has become more complex, so my

ethics have been called upon to guide me in the roles of leader and follower in a modern-day corporation. In one way or another, whether in a family, government, business, or college, each of us is clearly at different times a leader and a follower. Just as clearly, we always move in a time of new realities.

I was introduced to new realities back in the mid-sixties. I was teaching at Aquinas College in Grand Rapids a night class for young managers. In the group was the superintendent of a small company. He told me that the owner of the company, though uncomfortable out on the plant floor, made it a practice to approach people personally after they had worked for the company for a year. The owner would walk right into the plant, give a short speech to the first-year employee, and then produce a really beautiful symbol, the company's logo, on a sterling-silver tie tack, all presented in a velvet box. One day the owner was out in the plant giving his speech to a young man who had recently completed his first year. The young man opened the box, took out this wonderful sterling-silver tie tack, and said, "Gee, that's beautiful!" Then he calmly inserted it into the lobe of his left ear.

Twenty-five years ago, that was a new reality. There are new realities for leaders today spawned by technology, the mere size of organizations, and the unavoidable complexity of human relationships. Leaders and followers—remember everybody plays both positions—live today with the tension between words and behavior. Our daily context is one of words. Global communications threaten to enslave us to media. Our need to achieve often leads us to worship an agenda. The complexity of our relationships often makes it tempting for us to rely on the mere words of proliferating journals and manuals. Much of this is inevitable, and it creates for leaders, I believe, a real difficulty. You see, when we're effective leaders, our performance is normally based on such things as trust and vision and competence and fidelity. Most of us understand these things through observing behavior, not by reading books or listening to speeches. That's the case if you're a CEO, an attorney, a parent, or a teacher. This, I believe, is a truism.

In the fall of 1989, our country had the honor of hosting Lech Walesa. When he addressed the United States Congress, he said something that almost went unnoticed in our country. He was speculating about how Americans were going to respond as a nation to the astounding events in Eastern Europe. Walesa said many memorable things. One is especially relevant here. He said, "There is a declining world market for words."

I doubt that Congress had heard that before, and it probably doesn't believe it. Ethics and leadership always join in behavior. Our voices, our words, are essential but in vain without action. I don't believe, though, that ethics is a list of prohibitions. Nor is ethics a list of things we can get away with. I believe that ethical people know what is right and do what is right. The challenge for leaders, it seems to me, is how and where to apply our beliefs to the daily stream of interactions with other people.

Peter Drucker taught many years ago the difference between being effective and being efficient. Efficiency is doing something right; effectiveness comes from doing the right things. We only get to do the right thing well when the quality of our relationships transcends the pressures of the day-to-day and the realities of being human.

Three ideas light up for me the intersection of ethics and leadership—justice, celibacy, and the common good.

1. Ethical leadership withers without justice. Leaders refine themselves and improve their organizations in the crucible of public action. Justice may be the most important quality in the eyes of followers; unjust leaders paralyze their followers. Thus a primary responsibility for the just leader is to provide a level playing field, so that the game can be played. Let me give you a few thoughts— there are many more—about the application of justice.

We can think about justice as governing the distribution of results. People used to talk about the distribution of wealth. I think today we have a problem distributing results.

Many years ago, Herman Miller's board of directors decided that if we were going to think seriously about relationships in the workplace, we would have to deal with very real matters. The first was the relationship between the individual and the corporation as expressed in compensation. As a result, for more years than I can now remember, the CEO's cash compensation has been limited to an amount twenty times the average annual compensation of a factory worker. It establishes a credible basis for relationships. I'll add that there's no magic in the number twenty, but over the years it seems to have worked out. To me, it says that community results from justice, not from quantification.

Justice requires that leadership be a posture of indebtedness. Leaders need to ask themselves the question, "What do I as a leader owe?" Think, for instance, of the leader's obligation to provide first for those on the bottom rung, not for those on the top rung. To me, that's antithetical to the way in which much of capitalism works today. Perhaps even the metaphor misleads us. Ladders represent hierarchy, only one of the structures available to an effective leader.

To make justice a guiding force in our lives and in relationships requires that we scrutinize our communications. Communications in families, corporations, churches, colleges—any institution—can never be effective or just unless they can and do stand up to examination from leaders and followers. When I started working at Herman Miller, all one hundred people there knew everybody else by first name. Now over five thousand people work for Herman Miller, and it's difficult to stay in touch. As CEO, I required each member of my work team, six of us, to meet once a month with no agenda with twelve to fifteen volunteers for at least an hour over a meal. It's amazing what you can learn when you don't have an agenda. It's tough for some hard-driving vice presidents to go into meetings without agendas, but it can be done.

One day, in one of those sessions, Nancy Honor, relatively new to the company, asked me why I didn't believe in adoption. I told her that I did believe in adoption. (It can be a little disconcerting to listen to somebody else tell you what you believe!) She continued, "No, you don't. If you thought adoption was okay, the company would pay for it the way they do for a natural birth." Well, you know, I didn't realize that the company didn't pay for adoptions. I also didn't know that adoptions cost as much and sometimes more than a natural birth. It took us about two weeks to change the policy.

Another lesson I learned from this experience is that organizations communicate whether a leader plans it or not. The best, sometimes the only, way to discover just exactly what is being communicated is to make it possible for followers to tell you. (See "Ropes or Bathrooms" for more about this.)

2. A second connection between ethics and leadership, I like to call celibacy. I grew up in a strongly Protestant family. I thought for most of my early years that celibacy had to do with sexual abstinence. Then one day a friend introduced me to Dutch theologian Henri Nouwen's writings. In devouring his great book *Clowning in Rome* I learned that celibacy really has to do with making room for God. We need to make room for a number of things as leaders.

We need to make room for the stewardship of limited resources. We do not live in a world of unlimited resources of any kind, and we need to deal ethically with that problem. You know that minerals and oil are limited, but let's go on from there. What about the needs of most of the world's families? It seems to me that in addition to water, food, shoes, and so forth we need to think about health and education, hope and freedom.

Leaders exemplify personal restraint in their behavior. It is a matter of making room for more meaningful things in our lives. Two members of the University of Southern California faculty, Warren Bennis and Ian Mitroff, have written a marvelous book called *The Unreality Industry*. They sum up the need for personal restraint fairly well. Western societies are threatened, they say, by "their own self-inflicted, endless pursuit of mindless pleasures and trivialities, e.g., drugs, TV, the endless consumption of junk food, useless material items, and trivializing ideas." That's not a very appealing picture of our society. How to discover the ethics of simplicity in our capitalist system has become a serious problem.

Leaders make room for the family, their own and the families of the people they lead. How can a leader learn to think about the family as the special thing that it is? Thirty-five years ago I was lucky enough to learn how to do that. I was a very young manager, and driving home from church one Sunday evening, I told Esther, my wife, that Monday was going to be a difficult day. We were going to have to lay off forty men. (In those days, with only a couple of women in the office and three or four seamstresses in the upholstery department, we always talked about everybody as men.) She said quietly, "You don't have that right." As usual, I was slow to see the wisdom in what she said and told her again that we would probably lay off forty men the next day. Patiently she explained, "You're not thinking about that correctly, you're talking about laying off forty families."

Since then, I have never been able to think about individuals in the workplace without thinking also of their families. You see, leaders are accountable for intervening in organizational processes on behalf of the family.

3. *Ethics and leadership intersect in the common good.* A man I worked with years ago used to sting me with a saying that he always meant in a humorous way: "What good's happiness? You can't buy money with it." That thinking runs through so much of the capitalist system, a system overburdened with a desire to quantify the short-term payback to individuals. I'd like to suggest three ways to consider the common good. You'll surely be able to add more.

Leaders learn how to become abandoned to the needs of the followers. The needs of the followers can never be at odds with the true interests of a leader. What are some of the needs of followers? Think about yourself as a follower for a minute. You need competence and reality. You need from your leader compassion and fairness. You need a leader who's visible and whose life exemplifies fidelity. You need the right opportunity, and to reach your potential, you need somebody to give you the gift of accountability. We need somebody who will give us a chance to reach for our potential, and we need somebody who does not fear truth—seeing it, accepting it, and telling it!

Leaders learn how to make a commitment to the common good. One of the productive tenets of capitalism is the idea of individual opportunity, or individual right. When you think ethically about this, individual freedom becomes difficult to justify unless it results ultimately in the common good. I think there's a lot of evidence in our system today which makes that clear. If we're going to defend the common good, we need to understand that it doesn't work on the trickle-down theory. We will progress toward the common good only if we as individuals are intentional about pursuing it.

Leaders aspire to look like small boys in August. If you raise children or grandchildren, you know that by the end of August, they've been running around all summer in their shorts, sneakers, and T-shirts. You also know that their knees and their elbows are always skinned, their shins always black and blue, and that they have the marks of the summer's fracases on their faces. A six-year-old boy at the end of August is my picture of a leader.

I got that picture from David Hubbard, president of Fuller Theological Seminary in Pasadena. Many years ago he told me that leaders need to learn not to inflict pain, but to bear pain. It seems to me that if you're bearing pain properly as a leader, whether you're a preacher, a college professor, a parent, or a teacher, you ought to have the marks of the struggle. One ought to have bruised shins and skinned knees.

At the beginning of this chapter I asked, when do a leader's ethical beliefs cross her commitments to an organization? I think that the answer is this: A leader's commitments and beliefs are part and parcel of the same thing. A true leader cannot commit herself without beliefs. But in composing voice and touch, action must follow closely a solid sense of one's ethics.

Give the Gift of Change

.....

In Anglo-Saxon and Norse cultures, a leader established a reputation in large part by the quality of his gifts to his followers and visitors. Kings and princes gave gifts to welcome their friends and strengthen their alliances. So it is in or-

ganizations today, but I would like you to think of
gifts in a slightly different way.

Some gifts to ponder:

- Space—to be the kind of person I can be.

- Opportunity—to serve.

- Challenge—constraints are enabling friends.

- Clarity—in objectives, in evaluation, and in
  feedback.

- Authenticity—that gives hierarchy its true
  value, that gives me the right to offer my
  gifts, that neither overlooks nor oppresses.

- Meaning—a lasting foundation for hope.

- Accountability—a result of love

- Conscience—that forbids people to enjoy
  apathy or debilitating ease.

There is one last gift I would like to discuss
with you for the rest of this chapter, an ethos for
change. One can accept the reality and preva-
lence of change, but what next? How can I create
a culture for change?

As I have said in other parts of this book, some
thinking must come first. Principles must guide a

leader in managing change positively, effectively, and gracefully. Please don't underestimate the power of grace.

- It's important that we focus more on what we need to be than on what we need to do. In so doing, leaders do transform people's lives. What a daunting responsibility!

- The quality of our relationships is the key to establishing a positive ethos for change. Long-lived and productive relationships spring up from a soil rich in covenants and trust.

- An ethos for change derives its vitality from vision-based change. People follow easily the leader who undertakes meaningful changes clearly connected to a strategy. This is not always easy, but I've never looked on ease as an incentive.

- Leaders see that an organization's capacity to change depends to a great degree on effective followership.

- When unusual people and ideas are welcome, there is an ethos for change. To persuade their organizations to be open and vulnerable to unexpected results, leaders first open themselves. Leaders know who gives an organization health, who waters the roots of renewal.

The work of bringing about change is a leader's work. Naturally there are risks. And there are tensions. The tensions and our understandable fear of them often inhibit an organization's ability to welcome change. I'd like to suggest some sources of these tensions. Perhaps by understanding the sources, we can moderate some of the tension around change.

- A lack of preparation.

- Our complete inability to control change. We are swept along by huge and irresistible global events, mysteries, and movements.

- The warm comfort of routine.

- An ignorance of the reasons for change.

- Difficulty in separating self from issue. Our basic values and beliefs don't change every time the organization changes direction. Yet it will always be hard for the people truly involved in the life and work of an organization to divorce completely self from issue.

- The inability to reconcile events with values.

- The necessity of raising the level of trust.

- The problem of balancing individual needs and the common good. This shouldn't surprise anyone. All societies have this difficulty. Yet I believe that the legitimacy of individual freedom lies in the common good as well as in the dignity of persons.

- Braving the black gulf of the unfamiliar.

- The need to exercise both patience and guts. A leader must drive for action while tolerating inaction, a perfect formula for personal tension.

- Determining how much change a person and a family and an organization can digest. A very few people seem to know this limit instinctively.

Understanding the sources of the tension around change will not remove all risk. An unwillingness to accept risk has swamped more leaders than anything I can think of. Yet risk, like change, is natural, predictable, and to be welcomed. Ask yourself these questions about change and the risks of change:

- Will the change and the risk get us any closer to fulfilling our mission and realizing our vision?

- Will the hoped-for result be appropriate?

- Is the goal worth the cost? Where will we put the bodies? Can I achieve both progress and reconciliation?

- Am I careful not to condemn the past by my change?

- I myself may be willing to take enormous risks, but can I ask in good conscience others to share in those risks?

- Do I have a reasonable chance of succeeding? Are we playing to our strengths? Will the change help us reach our potential?

- How accurate are my perceptions? Has an idea become a moral conviction with me and, therefore, something the group and I can no longer look at objectively or negotiate?

- Have I allowed progress to become more important than spiritual growth and community?

- Do I ever lapse into a pursuit of change for its own sake? Do I ever lose sight of why I'm taking a risk?

- Am I alert to the distinction between loyalty and competence? Between conservation and change?

- Am I prepared to confront and evaluate the results of risk and change?

The last step, ideally—and I do realize that change is often upon us before we know it—is to implement the change. There are many ways of implementing change. Implementing change, like leadership and like music, is more an art than a science. I do believe leaders ought to follow some guidelines.

Leaders are visible. They do not sit safely in an ivory tower, whether the tower is on a campus or in a corporate headquarters. Leadership is not an arm's-length proposition. Followers have a right to *see* their leaders.

Leaders understand the context in which people work. Do you know who's who and what's what? Or do you only think you know? Another way to put this is to ask yourself whether you have a clear eye for reality.

A leader's actions incarnate an organization's beliefs and values. Remember that a truism gets to be that way because it is true: Actions do speak louder than words. Manuals don't count. Leadership is good work, not simply good talk.

Lavish communication is crucial. Change is a learning process. The score for change, the cadence that the organization is being asked to perform during a change, must be communicated consistently and redundantly. Leaders and followers must be literate.

The right of scrutiny belongs to each participant. Diversity is expressed through scrutiny and criticism; diversity, when made manifest, strengthens the process of change. It is the avenue to a group's true potential.

Let me end this chapter with a story to illustrate some of what I've been talking about. A little reality always brings abstractions down to earth for me and makes them more meaningful. Change really is a gift to be given. Leading and managing change is a gift to be developed.

While CEO of Herman Miller (and one assumes certain rights and privileges as the CEO), I arrived at work one morning with a long list of telephone calls to be made. As I turned to my telephone, I discovered that my old phone with its thirty-six familiar buttons had been replaced by a gadget with an LCD display that looked like nothing I had ever touched before. I asked my executive assistant what this gadget was and found out that it was, in fact, my new telephone.

"But I didn't ask for a new telephone," I said. "Well," Carol responded, "Everybody's got one." At 3 P.M., I was to be trained in its operation. I asked Carol if she could speed things up. I had a lot of work to do.

Within a few minutes, Sally arrived and told me cheerfully that she was here to teach me how to use my new phone. Her first question was "Are you computer literate?" I wasn't. "Can you read the instructions on the screen?" Well, I couldn't. She turned up the brightness. I still couldn't read the thing. "In that case," she said—remember, I'm the CEO—"perhaps you can't have a telephone."

When I asked for my old phone back, Sally told me it had already been junked. At this point, I was becoming a little perturbed. I really didn't want to change to a phone that rang with the tune "Mary Had a Little Lamb." Carol, sensing that warfare was about to erupt, stepped in and said she would work on the problem. Sally left.

A few hours later, a young man walked into my office, where I was holding a meeting. As if we weren't there, he lay down on the floor and began to work on the cabling of the new telephone. I inquired as civilly as I could what he was doing. He told me in a matter-of-fact way, "Sally said you didn't want a telephone that rings 'Mary Had a Little Lamb,' and I'm changing it to 'The Battle Hymn of the Republic.' "

Believe me, when no one paves the way, change is tough to take. I certainly wasn't prepared for this change, and I must admit that since I continued for the rest of the day as CEO, I managed to get my old phone back.

Delegate!
.....

During World War II, I worked as a medical technician and scrub nurse for Col. Luther Carpenter, an outstanding surgeon. One weekend when most of the staff were on leave in Paris, a young man was brought into the hospital with a critically fractured skull. Colonel Carpenter asked me to assist him in the surgery that had to take place immediately. No other surgeons were on duty.

Colonel Carpenter coolly explained that two things would have to happen simultaneously. He would clear the pieces of broken skull, while I would find the membrane that covers the back of the hamstring muscle, remove a four-inch piece, and repair the incision. He would use this very tough membrane to protect the patient's brain. I had never done something like this before, and you can imagine my alarm. But Colonel Carpenter was not fazed. "You've been working in this operating room for more than a year. You've seen all of this, and you've even done some small parts of it yourself. I'll be right here giving you instructions."

The operation was a success. The colonel was right. Clear instruction, confidence expressed as a high expectation, and an obvious trust in my ability to do the job. This was one of my earliest lessons in delegation.

Much has been written about delegation, most of it, unfortunately, by folks who do not have to practice delegation as a matter of effectiveness or survival. Hard-driving business managers are often too suspicious to abandon themselves to the consequences of real delegation. They trap themselves into dumping rather than delegating. College presidents and deans sometimes feel delegation is antithetical to collegial relationships. Clergy often see delegation as a shirking of their duty rather than a gracious act of involvement. Jazz-band leaders know it for what it is.

I believe we need to think more carefully about what delegation ought to bring to our own—and others'—career development, to our personal journey, to the need to involve those with special gifts. We need to ask ourselves what delegation ought to accomplish in the work of our organizations. The good work of leadership requires us to think seriously about the art of delegation and to practice that art diligently.

As I often do, I begin by asking questions. We

can ask several as we think about delegation. As with most of my lists, I hope you will add your own items.

What exactly is delegation? To be a good leader and a poor delegator is a contradiction in terms. Delegation is one of the ways for a leader to connect voice and touch. It is a precious way of enabling people to participate, to grow, to reach toward their potential.

It is the best process for personal development because it gives people the opportunity to learn by doing, to take risks, and to become comfortable with the consequences of their own performance. One cannot reach her potential without this process.

Delegation is central to participation and growth, to working and being accountable. Through delegation, leaders give their witness in the active practice of beliefs. Delegation is one kind of legitimate participation. Delegation is both an essential organizational function and an important gift to followers.

Like other aspects of the work of leadership, delegation is a serious, high-risk, and high-potential meddling in other people's lives. It demands thorough preparation and a loving commitment. We reveal clearly our attitude in the way in which we delegate. A good leader says, "I love you enough to make you accountable. You have the right to be part of this task."

What does delegation require? It's not easy to delegate well in the hurly-burly of organized life. Delegation requires careful observation, layers of skill, much feedback, and of course some failure. There is a format to follow. We can't practice true delegation with a lick and a promise. Good delegation is not something leaders do ad hoc. It's a rigorous, disciplined part of being a leader. Goals and assumptions are required. There are the needs of the delegate to be met. There are constraints and results.

I am sure you can add to the process I would like to outline, but I don't believe you can delegate effectively and take a shortcut.

155

Delegation requires that leaders adopt certain goals, goals that require us to think of achievement as a collaborative and synthetic result. We need both efficiency and effectiveness. Personal development and growth must accompany meeting the organization's needs. Another two-faceted goal is continuing education and succession planning (which I will talk about later in greater detail).

Delegation is one way of dealing with the increasing complexity in organizations. Obviously one reason to delegate is to get the work done, done well and done on time. It seems to me that this goal is impossible to meet—that it is impossible for a modern-day organization to reach its potential—until through delegation a leader brings to bear the diverse gifts of many individuals.

When I think about delegation, I make some important assumptions. It seems to me that diversity consists of our individual gifts and that the spectrum of gifts gives organizations strength. I also know that every leader has limitations; no one person can be all things to the organization. Any leader who limits her organization to the talents and time of the leader seriously handicaps the group.

I'm also assuming that the process of delegation, like most of a leader's work, depends heavily on the quality of our relationships. We become corporately effective by trusting that others can do some things better than we can. This is a risk, of course, in terms of the organization, but I see it as a natural and essential risk.

If you agree with me in these assumptions, you'll agree that as the complexity of organized life increases, delegation is really our only hope. I don't know of any alternative. There simply isn't a better way to skin a cat than by capitalizing on the human gifts that come to an organization.

Back to what delegation requires of a leader. As I see it, delegation requires a form of dying, a separation of issue from self. We must surrender or abandon ourselves to the gifts that other people bring to the game. We must become vulnerable to every person's need for the opportunity to do her best. Machinery and materials and buildings acquire a kind of personality of their own; people intimate with such inanimate things develop a kind of relationship with them. This means to me that we must go beyond learning a single skill or specific knowledge to acquiring the art and grace of a job. Knowing how to thread a needle doesn't make a seamstress.

While good delegation requires a form of dying, it is also the only way for leaders to stay alive. A friend of mine, team-teaching with me one day, told the class that the alternative to good delegation was for him a nervous breakdown. Surely when leaders delegate poorly or not at all, they take health away from organizations and fail to move real contributors toward their potential.

Delegation requires that a leader clearly state the corporate vision, a vision to be fully shared and discussed and scrutinized. Understanding and acceptance must follow. Only then can leaders enroll followers in advocacy. Note that I said "acceptance" and not "agreement." In our adult lives, we all do many things without agreeing in every detail. In organizations, even if we don't completely agree, we have to accept a broad direction so that we become advocates and allow the organization to do its job. We must embrace the idea that corporate interests come before self-interests. (I'd like to add that I mean interests, not necessarily goals.)

Delegation, like much of a leader's work, requires trust. Trust begins at the top, when the leader speaks the truth and acts in accordance with beliefs. Trust results only when a leader keeps her promises. (See "A Key Called Promise.") Trust will never be a "fast track" proposition. It is the network of our interdependence. Leadership and followership are ideas linked by a trust that puts everyone at peace with ineluctable risk.

Delegation requires leaders to bring delegates a clear statement of expectations, to enumerate the job's goals and requirements. A leader must give responsibility and accountability and explain the risks. This makes the avenue of delegation a two-way street: Each party needs to be able to grow. As someone once said, in delegating, leaders give roots and they give wings.

The role of expectations is an astonishing thing. Expectations really can help people reach their potential. When the talented architects Eero Saarinen and John Dinkeloo designed the John Deere corporate headquarters in Moline, they brought in a first design to chairman and CEO Bill Hewitt. The site was a lovely oak woods out in the Illinois countryside. Bill told them that while he thought this design was a fine piece of work, he also thought that they could produce something more inspired. (Of course, Bill was really saying that he had higher expectations of people with Saarinen's and Dinkeloo's talents.) The two architects returned with truly an inspired design, a building constructed of Cor-Ten steel that blended naturally into the rust-colored oak woods.

What do delegates need? First, they need a defined purview. They need to know their authority and accountability. They need to know how much "turf" is involved. They need to know the who, what, and when of the project, not the how —that is what the delegate brings. They need all the information the leader has and the sum of a leader's wisdom regarding the project. Good delegation clearly implies that the leader become a mentor.

The delegate also needs to have certain agreements with a leader. Together they will define reality, establish the validity of the mission, understand and accept the work to be done. They need to state their goals. They need to come to terms about the potential for growth and the way to measure performance. Last but not least, they need to discuss failure. How should they react if the project fails?

The delegate has personal needs. She needs from the leader a high degree of clarity and access. She needs to be assured that she will have the leader's time and involvement at certain stages of the project. She needs to hear the leader give her the chance to grow, to achieve, to do her best, to take risks, and to fail. She needs to be certain that the leader is committed to her success.

It would be hard to overestimate the importance of lavish communication throughout the process of delegation. Leaders encourage their delegates, both through words and behavior. Leaders educate delegates as a way of giving meaning and direction and literacy to the process. Leaders liberate delegates through communication and enable them to respond to the demands of responsibility. The leader's communication will be effective only if it is scrutinized and questioned, challenged and clarified. The kind of communication I'm talking about includes chances for review. The leader and delegate need opportunities to evaluate how things are going, to look out for the signs of entropy. Leaders coach and connect without assuming responsibility or accountability or a share of the work. Leaders delegate completely or not at all.

The dictionary often helps me see things clearly. It defines a delegate as one "sent *and empowered.*" It seems to me that we all too many times concentrate on the first and forget about the second. The definition of the verb delegate includes this: "to *entrust* to another." Jazz!

What are the constraints? And I think of constraints as friends, as something natural to the process of delegation and the entire good work of leadership. Constraints can give us important limits to life within which to operate. They can even give us clues as to how we can go beyond complexity toward simplicity in solving problems. A key constraint in delegation is the requirement to get something done. This constraint chafes against people who enjoy what I call perpetual fact gathering. While this constraint may entail an imperfect result, we do have to move to closure. There is much to be said for completion.

Leaders cannot delegate everything. They must

bear the responsibility for picking the delegate. And leaders cannot delegate their own responsibilities. A good friend, an avid sailor, once hosted three guests from England for a weekend. While talking about what to do, the guests expressed an interest in sailing. My friend asked them if they were experienced sailors, they answered yes, and he invited them to borrow his boat. After showing them around the boat and pointing out the equipment, he returned to his house, where he discreetly watched the proceedings. Without untying the boat, the three raised the sail into a stiff breeze. My friend immediately walked to the dock and suggested that he go along.

Leaders keep the same ground rules over the course of the work. Naturally some things may change during a project, but the basic assumptions under which a delegate is working don't change.

A delegate is constrained to keep the leader informed. This benefits both the leader and the delegate. It builds their relationship and lets the delegate learn from the leader. Of course, the leader must make herself available.

Leaders are constrained to accept the results of delegation and deal with them. Whether the results turn out to be spectacularly bad or especially successful, a leader is responsible for the delegating. The leader who delegates cannot become an absentee landlord.

What do we do with the results of delegation? First, of course, we say thank you. Then we give recognition to the delegate within the organization. These two things seem obvious to me.

Next, we have to deal with rewards. Symbolism is essential but never sufficient.

Honest evaluation of the results, a vital part of personal growth, must follow. Leaders have to confront failure as well as success. Failure is a natural part of work in organizations, and we should treat it that way. You might even say that people who never fail have not been trying hard enough —or have sailed their boats in small and perpetually calm ponds.

Last, a leader will recognize that a new challenge best rewards a successfully completed project or good performance.

As necessary and as effective as true delegation seems to be, it does not occur automatically. It is one of the most precious gifts leaders must choose to give. It may remain a gift that goes ungiven. It's up to you.

Polishing Gifts

·····

Opportunities for developing one's leadership and managerial abilities abound. Most concern one's career and focus on corporate or institutional needs. Since the corporation or the institution is paying the bill, this probably makes sense. It may not be enough, however, for you as an individual.

The organization assumes that you'll be sticking to a career track for life. Maybe that's true, but maybe it isn't. The organization seldom asks what your spouse thinks, or what your life plan might be, or whether the organization's direction really aligns with what you consider to be your gifts.

We and our families need to think seriously about long-term potential and opportunity. We need to take into account not only the needs of our careers, but the "careers" of every member of our families. We need to focus on those areas of extracurricular service that provide us health. We need to be aware that many organizations too easily dispense with persons. We need to be aware that the United States is a nation of volunteers; city councils and hospital boards and school boards need leaders just as badly as institutions.

Leaders polish all their facets equally. Developing one's career alone won't be enough for leaders. Communities and organizations need different things from leaders, qualities that must be nurtured and grown simultaneously. Leaders think about polishing their personal gifts. And it has always seemed to me that crystals with many facets shine brightest.

Polishing gifts differs from career development. Though many people will be ready to help you reach your potential, you must act first. Leaders see a twofold opportunity—to build a life and to build a career. And the fact is that people become leaders only by building both.

Polishing gifts is a family affair, not an individual event. You might even think of it as an amateur event. I hope that it will come naturally to you to see polishing gifts in the light of your contribution to the common good as opposed to accumulating for yourself experiences and goods. Leaders deal in substance and the quality of life, deaf to the calls to pursue quantity and appearances.

Leadership is a job, not a position. The people

who work with you are not your people; you are theirs. Leadership is good work because leaders feel a strong need to express their potential and because they wish to serve the needs of others. This is the essence of becoming a "servant leader."

Good leaders know that moving up in the hierarchy does not magically confer upon them competence. They know that being elected president, for instance, gives them the *opportunity to become* president. Leaders also know that their real security lies in their personal capabilities, not in their power or position.

A leader's capabilities begin to be tested shortly after she arrives on the job. Spontaneity and reflection begin to fade away amid the din of schedules leaders don't make and commitments they don't seek out. Required reading begins to edge out elective reading. More and more energy goes into resisting pressure to move in undesired directions. Truly, serving as a leader is a trying vocation.

Polishing gifts begins by reflecting on how to design the ways in which you as a leader or future leader will work intelligently toward your potential. In talking about polishing gifts, I'm not talking about putting one's faith in self-improvement. Nor am I suggesting that on a higher level we can become whatever we choose to be. That would run counter to the convictions of my Christian faith. I do believe leaders can share some guidelines, can direct their thinking, and can heed some notes of caution in considering their roles as leaders of families, institutions, and communities. Still, with all the guidelines in the world, polishing gifts can be risky: You may change.

Some years ago, my wife and three of our children and I were fortunate to spend a week's vacation in Morocco. One day we decided to do some shopping in the souk in Marrakech. Shopping in a north African souk is a lot like becoming a CEO —you can't know ahead of time exactly what you're getting into.

As we approached the entrance, a young man

with an official guide badge offered his services. A relatively seasoned traveler, I thanked him and said we really wanted to be on our own. After about an hour, we began to realize that we were seeing some areas for a second and third time. Nevertheless, when the young man approached us again, I gave him the same answer, and he slipped back into the crowd. After another hour or so, we were absolutely and hopelessly lost. This time the young man had a big smile on his face and said, "You need me, no?" We welcomed him with open arms.

Polishing gifts is much like shopping in the souk—it's very difficult to do without help.

In thinking about polishing gifts, we probably need the most help at the starting point. How do we understand our own gifts and limitations? How can we identify and measure and evaluate them?

Followers adamantly demand that a leader possess a high degree of integrity when it comes to self-perception. A combination of self-confidence and humility seems to me to be crucial, for this oxymoronic quality makes it possible for the group to be decisive. Organizations have a right to expect decisiveness from leaders. Being decisive in an area of one's strengths is not too difficult. As important as an awareness of one's limitations is, it can never scotch one's willingness to act. Acting in the face of one's weakness requires courage and risk—symbiotic abstractions brought to reality with the assistance of self-confidence and, of course, with the assistance of those with whom we work.

Polishing gifts requires us to think broadly and deeply and to develop our voice, to understand what we believe. Until we examine our perceptions of ourselves, we can't really know who we are and what our gifts really are. What and how do we see? Do we have a philosophy—or even a theology—of life? Do matters of culture mean something to us? Are we willing to develop an interest in literature and architecture and the arts? Are we comfortable with thinking about relationships parochially, or have we begun to think cross-culturally? Do we signal to others that it's okay to offer suggestions?

I remember so clearly the time I spent in basic training at Camp Grant, Illinois, during World War II. In the course of training, I did something that caught the attention of the battalion commander and was ordered to appear in his office the next morning at eight o'clock.

The evening before, the second lieutenant, whom I knew only casually, called me out of the barracks. "They won't tell you this at headquarters," he said, "but I want you to know that in the morning they're going to offer you the opportunity to go to officer candidate school." He went on to tell me that I wouldn't have to explain if I declined, but if I did decline, they would call me back after a week and offer to send me to college. "I just think you should know ahead of time what the choices are," he said.

This was for me a life-changing event. I chose to go to college. The army responded by sending me to several, including the Sorbonne. I've always hoped that the lieutenant realized how important his intervention was in my life.

Polishing gifts requires from us, and teaches us, that we need to learn to think in terms of discovery. Polishing gifts often removes years of routine and the accumulated layers of habit. Who knows what we will find underneath! Once a discovery is made, it's up to us to make the connections, to give the discovery a relevance to our present situations.

In thinking about polishing gifts, we need to be directed both internally and externally. Let me give you a few questions I ask myself.

- How do I learn best? By reading or listening or through conversation? What is it that triggers me?

- What settings or groups lead to my most productive times? For most people, I think, the best way to learn is to become actually involved in risky work. We need to be given serious work to do, to carry full responsibility and accountability for failure and success. (This, I believe, is one reason delegation is such an important part of a leader's job. She

Leadership Jazz
· · · · ·

must train successors in actual combat. (See
"Delegate!")

- How do I feel about working with a mentor?
A mentoring relationship is one of the best
ways to discover one's gifts and weaknesses.
Remember that a learning leader must seek
out her mentors and maintain the relationship. Mature mentors understand that advice should be given only when it has been
requested.

- Am I willing to reserve time on my calendar
for reflection?

- Have I thought about writing down the
things in my own life and that of my family
that I want to measure?

- In learning to listen, have I thought about
improving my ability to practice the art of
silence? It is an art widely underrated and
too little understood. Do I listen with an
intent to learn, to feel, to understand, to
see?

- What do my family and I need to cultivate
to reach our potential?

Some years ago, I arranged a series of seminars
for senior managers at Herman Miller. We studied
government for two days with Senator Mark
Hatfield. We gained a perspective on the world

social order from E. F. Schumacher, author of
Small Is Beautiful. We learned about leadership
development from Robert Greenleaf. We studied
world economics under Irving Kristol. We studied
leadership and corporate growth with Peter
Drucker, and, of course, with Peter we also
learned about Japanese art, music, economics, and
history. The purpose of these sessions was not to
teach us business management but to offer us an
opportunity to broaden and deepen ourselves and,
through us, our families.

Good leadership includes teaching and learning, building relationships and influencing people,
as opposed to exercising one's power.

- How am I going to nourish the spiritual, the
  visionary, the musical, the childlike side of
  my nature? How am I going to minimize the
  stale, mechanical, quantifiable side of my
  life?

- Where will I find the discipline to visit museums, to read good literature, to learn about
  music, to understand architecture, to go on a
  picnic?
  A great way to begin to think cross-cul-

turally is to visit the Girard Wing of the Museum of International Folk Art in Santa Fe, New Mexico. By studying folk art, one sees the essential patterns of life across many cultures. Folk art celebrates the passages of life from birth through death. It celebrates faith and worship, the lessons of community and of the gathered good. Folk art expresses the transfer of power and responsibility; it testifies to the role of beliefs and values over the generations. In short, the hundreds of years of folk art surely have much to teach us about what's important to modern institutions and to the work of leaders.

· Am I prepared to think about polishing gifts as a way of dealing with time and leaving a legacy? As the years slip by, am I learning to see through the lens of mortality? How does this improve me today as a leader?

· How am I going to learn to deal with the difference between speed and time? It seems to me that speed constantly threatens the legacy of leaders, forcing them to leave in their wake merely the debris of spoiled hopes, defeat, and meaningless acquisition. Somehow quality and substance, like truth, arise from an awareness of time. Leaders replace speed with time, by sitting by the fire, watching the embers, acquiring a rhythm and poise that last a lifetime. Georgia

O'Keeffe once said that seeing flowers, like friendship, takes time. So, too, with polishing gifts.

- What will give me joy at seventy or eighty? At the end of life, what will I face? Or, more important, whom?

- Where will I find the resources for stroking the arm of a dying loved one? Or for finding love for an elderly parent who has turned into a person I have never known? Or for discovering how much a place has changed since someone is no longer there? These kinds of questions face every person; leaders are certainly not exempt from them.

Let me make a few specific suggestions for starting to answer these questions and polishing one's gifts.

Make a parallel track for responsible work in your life, something that complements your career but also serves others. I think this helps leaders reach their potential.

Practice leadership without power. Serving on a school board or coaching tee-ball or volunteering in a hospice is an effective way to polish gifts.

Working in eleemosynary service has broadened my understanding of what it means to make a commitment to the common good.

Learn your language and use it with respect. This seems to me to be a characteristic of the best leaders. Does an ignorance of one's language make a leader a poor one? Or does being a poor leader result in a lack of respect for speaking and writing well?

Learn to communicate in public.

Participate regularly in an intellectual pursuit. I read and discuss all kinds of books with a very special group of ten friends. Since I'm the only one without a Ph.D., I'm sometimes a little daunted, and talking about books with these people is risky for me. But friendship, stimulation, balance, and the intellectual vigor of our discussions are certainly worth the risk.

Learn who and what gives you health.

Begin to ponder seriously ideas for a second—or third—career.

Ask yourself frequently, "What truly gives meaning to my life?" Are you happy with the answer?

In an effort to sum up this large topic of polishing gifts, one that I certainly haven't exhausted, let me briefly discuss a three-faceted problem that I think leaders especially face in polishing gifts.

A rising level of din threatens to drown out the voices urging us to do the good work of leadership, part of which is polishing gifts. This din takes the form of distractions, addictions, and institutional politics.

Complexity can become a distraction, though it is normal in organized life. By moving personally and organizationally toward restraint and simplicity, we give ourselves a chance. It really comes down to setting priorities, as banal as that phrase has become. It comes down to dealing with the substantive before the superficial, of dealing with the strategic before the stressful, of leaving a legacy instead of accumulated assets, of being able to find a balance in life that gives equal footing to family and service.

We must beware that wealth not supplant richness or faith, that administration not replace leadership, that presenters not take precedence over producers. We must be aware that poise is a fragile thing. I am amazed that faced with enormous problems of education, poverty, the economy, foreign trade, and world health, our government will, in a destructive collaboration with the media, grind to a halt for two or three weeks over the matter of a flag burning. This happens in corporations and colleges as well.

Addictions can be part of the cacophony. There are addictions to drugs and power, to alcohol and work. We can become addicted to television and materialism and pornography, to the egos and glitter of the sports-and-entertainment complex. Leaders know that some people become addicted to advocacy—no matter how good the cause. These addictions feed only the appetites, not the spirit. They are part of the din through which leaders must lead. Career development programs will not help you here.

Another part of the din drumming in the ears of leaders is the seemingly endless political maneuvering that inevitably takes up so much time and energy in organizations. Changing agreed-on priorities and directions, the negotiator's waltz, can be a deadly dance. Good leaders place agreements out in the fresh air, in the open, and thereby reduce both the urge and the appeal of constantly changing direction. It's essential that we give our witness in the presence of our peers.

I am speaking about these problems in a musical metaphor partly because of a note I recently received from a friend. Let me quote from it.

Got your letter yesterday. Then Ernie Caviani tuned the piano last night. In both cases, it was like hearing the real music again. Playing a piano after it has been tuned is a wonderful experience. The music is so clear and pure, with none of the dissident overtones that have built up as the strings slowly and inevitably go out of tune. Not only is each note sweet and clean, but so are the chords. I hauled out the pieces

I'm working on, and instead of wincing at the spots where the A-flat was driving me crazy, I relaxed as they sounded as Beethoven or Schubert had written them.

It seems to me that polishing gifts, such a crucial part of the work of a leader, could be called tuning oneself for life.

Amateurs

.....

A physician friend of mine once told me a story. As a young man, he had a patient, the owner of a small business, for whom he had performed beyond the call on more than one occasion. Physicians will often do that. The grateful patient invited the physician and his wife to the symphony and dinner as a small way of expressing his appreciation. At the concert, the conductor announced that the orchestra would perform for the first time a new composition by an American composer, and so it did. After the applause, much to my friend's surprise, the conductor looked at the young businessman, asked him to stand, and introduced him to the audience as the composer.

Was this young person an amateur composer and a professional businessman? Or was he a professional composer who ran a business for the love of it? Did his experience with balance sheets help his orchestration? Or did his knowledge of harmony enable him to listen for the music in a well-run organization? (If you have read *Leadership Is an Art,* you will remember similar questions about the millwright.) The answers to these questions can dazzle you with the especially bright light of human worth and human diversity.

I had the good fortune to hear Daniel Boorstin, the Librarian of Congress, speak to a design conference about amateurs and professionals. He calls himself, by the way, an amateur. And he includes among the ranks of amateurs true leaders. "The leader," he said, "is by definition an amateur— open to new vistas that training precludes from the professional." Perhaps he is right about leaders. I do know that leaders understand the important contributions that amateurs can make in organizations. Leaders make it possible for these sometimes difficult people to thrive and do their best.

Everyone relies on amateurs from time to time. When the official, professional channels clog up with bureaucratic sediment, people turn to amateurs for results. You go underground to get something done quickly and effectively. More often than not, if you go to the right amateur with the right problem, the action will be not only quick but effective.

For many reasons, some of them unarguable, organizations are by their nature antipathetic to amateurs. Only leaders can make it possible for amateurs to survive in organizations. They can do so by creating an attitude and environment that seeks out, empowers, and recognizes good ideas, no matter what the source. A leader makes it possible for a business person to be a composer. Leaders can make a college, a business, or any organization hospitable to the person without the usual credentials. The trick is simply to look at merit naked. Learn to hear the tune despite the noise.

To be an amateur means literally that you do something for the love of it. A love, a true love, of what you're doing results in real competence and real intimacy. An amateur is likely to forget about financial rewards; money for an amateur is more likely to be a result than a goal. In fact, money may even be an inappropriate reward. It's up to the real leaders in organizations to discover the right rewards for amateurs, an opportunity or a new challenge.

One characteristic of the amateurs I know is their curiosity. They like nothing better than learning something new. They are generally smart enough to recognize the limits of their knowledge and are constantly on the lookout for opportunities to expand those limits.

Some organizations take the word amateur to mean less than perfect. To perform consistently requires one to be a professional, say many people. And perhaps in our world, where knowledge and expertise have become so specialized and fragmented, they would often be right. Nobody would prefer to be treated by an amateur thoracic surgeon. I would say that organizations, like the old English cricket teams composed of "gentlemen and players," need both: Leaders would like to have some people who frequently exceed expectations and some people who never fall below them.

You'll find amateurs (though you may not call them that) at the heart of organizations already. By "heart," I don't mean "headquarters." Amateurs seem to be drawn to this frame of mind more easily than professionals. It's the gift of perception, not training.

Leaders make places for amateurs, for often am-

Leadership Jazz

ateurs have difficulty conforming even to the reasonable constraints of working in organizations. The strength of amateurs—their ability to fashion fresh solutions out of a sometimes naive curiosity —requires special nurturing, special teaching. The best leaders open themselves to the contributions of amateurs, though I must admit I have often worked hard to ignore or have simply tolerated the unorthodox methods of many good amateurs. It helps to remember that a group dominated by a leader will never exceed the talents of the leader.

Amateurs frequently contribute more when they don't join; they have a need to pledge a qualified allegiance. Far too many people are so addicted to organizations that they seldom question anything. Amateurs do not derive their security and identity from organizations but from their abilities; Sherlock Holmes is their patron saint. Though they are not afraid of losing their jobs, don't think of amateurs as disloyal. Amateurs are likely to be the most committed people around.

190

Their commitment may simply express itself in unusual ways.

Organizations have trouble evaluating the contributions of amateurs and placing them within the hierarchy. I don't find this surprising. In corporations functioning in a capitalist system, it is difficult to discard the yardstick of short-term financial gain. Profit, after all, is absolutely necessary for survival in a capitalist system. Profit gives us the chance to make a difference in the world, but profit is never more than a by-product. Peter Drucker calls profit the "cost of your future." I would like to consider motives and a broader view of performance. I happen to think that there is proof enough to convince even a cynic that amateurs working for the simple joy of it produce some pretty good results.

The unexpected result certainly comes from amateurs—the beneficial surprise. The unexpected has become anathema in a great many organizations. In some cases, rightly so. But think how often the odd juxtaposition, the unusual point of view, produces a stunningly elegant solution.

A few amateurs in the organization help such insights happen. I'm certain that at Herman Miller we came up with new ways of looking at things by trying hard to be hospitable as an organization to the unusual person and the offbeat point of view. At least we tried to give amateurs a chance to be heard.

How can we think about amateurs and places for them in organizations? How can leaders, especially, open their organizations to the influence of amateurs? How can leaders recognize the amateurs in their organizations and put them to good use?

I have a few ideas. Together with yours, we may have something.

Amateurs defy definition. They are often neither fish nor fowl. If Leonardo da Vinci, for example, were required to file a tax return, could he? What would he list as his occupation? Painter? Engineer? Scientist? In a large organization, where would he work? Graphic design? Development engineering? Research and design? Yet what leader would not wish to have a Leonardo somewhere on the team?

Being curious, amateurs sometimes run afoul of the organizational hierarchy. A leader will make it possible for a person occasionally to work outside the hierarchy. Colleges and universities do this through what they call "joint appointments." In fact, I would say that the effectiveness of amateurs is heightened when they are encouraged to cross traditional organizational boundaries.

A leader understands the importance of roving leaders, those indispensable people in our lives who take charge when we need them. Roving leaders fill vacuums. Amateurs often become roving leaders; their lack of fear allows them to step in and take charge. Amateurs simply don't know what they can't do. The familiar taboos of life in organizations don't frighten them. It is possible, however, for an organization to stifle the drive for accountability and good performance among amateurs.

Ideas, not authority, motivate amateurs. Authority truly motivates almost no one these days. It's
really more accurate to view employees as volunteers. Amateurs, especially, are mobile workers.
It's up to leaders to keep the ideas coming, to
prepare the ground where new ideas can grow.

And as you know, predictable answers grow in
most organizations like weeds, often choking out
an original idea. Amateurs don't automatically respect the predictable solutions to organizational
dilemmas. Their ignorance of the formula is of
great value.

People must be able to pursue their potential. Amateurs pursue their potential even under difficult
circumstances. Their work—in all its forms—expresses this pursuit. If an organization is wise
enough to attract amateurs and lucky enough to
keep them, creating an atmosphere where amateurs flourish becomes an important part of an
organization's life and values.

For leaders, carving out the room for people to
pursue their potential has many implications. In

my own life in business and in my attempts to become a better leader, I have asked myself the following questions:

- People have more than one dimension to their lives. Will my company allow people the freedom to express themselves in more than one way? Does my company help me find and use my gifts?

- Does the organization I work for allow people to build a relationship more positive than a simple contract? Are we free to make a covenant?

- Does my company place a higher value on ideas and deeds than on rank and reports?

- Are producers or presenters promoted? Are specialists *and* generalists recognized?

- Do the leaders in my organization pay more attention to the possibilities of the future than the honest mistakes of the past?

- Is it possible for the people who work here to have a hand in determining their future and their priorities?

- Does my organization honor what it cultivates?

Working in groups gives us a chance to deepen our lives and enlighten society. It gives us no chance, however, if we allow ourselves to build barriers that exclude more and more people as one looks at higher and higher echelons. As necessary as they are, the hierarchies of organizations are not the only ways to structure relationships or accountabilities. As vital as she is to the operation of institutions, the well-credentialed professional is not the only source of wisdom and insight.

Amateurs do not make life easy for leaders. And, of course, amateurs by themselves are not the only way to keep an organization vital or even merely functioning. Yet their willingness to object to the norm, learn frantically, and contribute in unexpected ways makes amateurs essential parts of organizations. Make a place for them.

Followership

·····

Like many companies, Herman Miller started out small and family-owned. My father, D.J., founded the company and for years was its president. My older brother Hugh had always been looked upon as D.J.'s successor in the family business and for seventeen years made a wonderful president. D.J. said more than once to me, "It takes more grace than tongue can tell to play the second fiddle well." I can surely attest to the truth in this. But I did learn something about leadership from trying to be a good follower.

While becoming a good follower is not the only way to become a good leader, it can be very important training. If one is already a leader, the lessons of following are especially appropriate. Leaders understand the essential contributions as well as the limitations of good followers. Experience in this case is the best teacher.

One obvious requirement for doing good work as a leader is to learn the perspective of followers. The first thing to remember: As long as a follower is in the group you lead, she is essential. Work teams, sports teams, and bands have this in common. I've often asked myself, "Are the poorest sandlot baseball players chosen last because they commit so many errors? Or do they commit errors because they're chosen last?"

When Herman Miller was building its base in Europe some years ago, key people would frequently move to Bath, England, for periods of time to help get the new company up and running. Roy Keech, an effective financial person whose avocation is playing the French horn, took his turn in that "green and pleasant land." As traveling people know, the weekends away from home are the longest.

While strolling through downtown Bath one Sunday, Roy came upon the park along the Avon River where the afternoon band concert was about to take place. He decided to join the crowd and listen. The band was late getting started, and when the conductor finally came to the podium, he announced that the French hornist wasn't there. They could not play their scheduled concert without a French horn. Could anyone in the audience fill in?

After waiting for someone else to volunteer and with great hesitation, Roy walked up to the conductor. He read through the music, picked up the band's French horn, practiced a few passages, and the concert went on. The audience appreciated the concert and Roy so much that the band ended the concert with "The Stars and Stripes Forever" to honor its new member from the States. The conductor, I imagine, had learned something about the fragility of leadership.

What can a leader learn by walking in the shoes of a follower?

- One quickly learns who delivers solutions and who loves to hand over problems.

- One learns that a leader needs to have a high threshold of pain and a low tolerance for what is popularly called BS.

- One learns to recognize the difficulty of holding people accountable while giving them space to make mistakes. One also learns the fundamental necessity of doing so.

- One learns that the story of the emperor and his clothes is more a parable than a fairy tale. If leaders are to stay dressed, they need a lot of help. Leaders cannot function without the eyes and ears and minds and hearts of followers.

- One learns the sometimes startling differences between the perceptions of leaders and the everyday realities of followers. Some months ago, one of the students at the seminary where I'm a member of the board of trustees asked the board, "If you want our help, do you know our needs? Do you know our gifts? Do you know our problems?"

- One learns that leaders only really accomplish something by permission of the followers.

- One finds out that in learning to play second fiddle well—and perhaps someday first fiddle —three questions come to mind: What does a follower owe? What should leaders beware of that inhibits good followership? What do followers need to know to keep their leader dressed?

Let's talk first about what followers owe. To be sure, leaders owe a great deal to their institutions and their followers. By the same token, followers owe a great deal to their institutions and their leaders. It is an issue of fairness, though, of what a leader can rightly expect. It seems to me, in the context of interdependent work, a leader has the right to expect followers to:

- Develop a high degree of literacy about the institution; understand its motives; know whom it serves; accept what must be measured and the constraints around the survival of the organization.

- Take responsibility for achieving personal goals; hold the organization responsible for providing a level playing field.

- *See* work and take ownership in areas consistent with their responsibilities and accountabilities. Connect themselves to those the organization ultimately serves.

- Become loyal to the idea behind the institution or business, even when unable to agree to all the goals and processes. (See "Amateurs.")

- Resist the inevitable and understandable fear of the unknown; realize that reality is not to be avoided.

- Understand the contributions of others and accept the authenticity of each member of the group.

- Make a personal commitment to be open to change.

- Take responsibility for civil and constructive relationships.

- Be a builder, not a taker.

- Ask a great deal of a leader. (I've discussed what kinds of questions followers might ask in "A Key Called Promise.")

What should leaders beware of that inhibits good followership? You could list hundreds of things that prevent people from being good followers, but I would like to mention a few basic elements. You can elaborate.

- Leaders can indulge in crimes of the spirit— cynicism, destructive criticism, unnecessary conflict, personal animosity, gossip—that create an atmosphere in which followers cannot survive, much less perform.

- Leaders who expect followers to be mind readers don't produce good second fiddlers; leaders cannot deprive followers of good training, good orientation, and access to necessary information without paying a price.

- A talented young woman with a bright future at Herman Miller left one day, much to my surprise, to work for a competitor. Sadly I called to wish her the best, and she promised to write to me explaining her decision. After some weeks, I received a long letter describing her failure to find a different position in Herman Miller that would allow her to use her gifts, that would give her the chance to advance and to reach her potential. For me, the key sentence in her letter was "I found several managers who said they wanted me, but nobody said they needed me." There is indeed an important difference: In the workplace, to be needed is the crucial condition.

- Change is essential to organizational survival. Followers are good at change when leaders are good at managing change.

- Leaders structure and practice involvement. They listen to, evaluate, and respond to input; they take action, or participation will not survive.

- Leaders are available to help, especially when it's painful.

- Leaders pay special attention to the equitable division of results. Nothing cankers the souls of followers like an unfair division of the spoils.

- Leaders do not indulge in imprudent and casual evaluations.

What is it that followers should know that will keep their leader dressed? A leader cannot—and should not—be aware of all the details in an organization. (Leadership is a lot like raising a seventeen-year-old. You don't need to know everything.) This, it seems to me, is both a great strength and an obvious weakness. It's up to the followers to fill in the gap.

- First, followers should know that they sabotage the entire organization by protecting the leader. Eliminate that fatuous phrase "no problem." For there *are* problems, and leaders exist to do hard work and be accountable for solutions to hard problems. A leader can do her best only in a truth-telling climate.

- The previous item suggests this one. Good followers don't withhold difficult options. Search for others' points of view. Seek out the "why" of each situation. Give the organization, through your leader, a chance at greatness.

- Don't forget that followers can improve their leader's ability to get the job done. Followers have a great deal to teach leaders. When Tom Davis, a respected veteran salesperson, retired from Herman Miller, I asked him what had given him the most satisfaction. He answered, "I surpassed my quota fif-

teen years running, and I successfully trained
five regional managers [his superiors!] in the
process."

I will never completely understand the relationship between leaders and followers. It can be
magical and health-giving or dispiriting and fatal.
Perhaps the most singular responsibility of followers is never to let their leader feel like a lion in a
den of Daniels. Performance of the group is the
only real proof of leadership.

Do Leaders Have a Future?

. . . . .

I was talking recently with a twenty-one-year veteran of Herman Miller about his future and about the quality of leadership that he could expect over the next fifteen years of his career. After all, he pointed out, "My family is in the hands of the corporation's leadership to a certain extent." He also felt a proprietary interest in the future of the company. "Remember," he said, "I'm a watercarrier now." Watercarriers are people in our company who have made a significant and consistent contribution to Herman Miller, an idea I've already talked about.

In the course of the conversation, I mentioned one vice president who had recently left, much to the relief of the organization, as a positive sign. He quickly countered, "That's my very point. You waited for him to quit. He should have been fired a year ago."

Our mistake was not in waiting too long to remove this person. It was in failing to select the right person in the first place or in helping this person too little to succeed. The selection, nurture, and assignment of people with senior responsibility is one of the most important and difficult and rewarding parts of a leader's job.

One of the myths of management is that good strategic planning and an appropriate vision will ensure an institution's future. I'm afraid this simply isn't enough. Only the effective selection, nurture, and assignment of senior people will secure an institution. When I ask myself about the future of an organization, this is my answer: Senior leaders *are* the future.

Senior leaders not only affect strategic thinking and planning, but they also shape an organization's vision and values and practices. Unconsciously and consciously, senior people leave their marks on an organization's culture and legacy.

As people are promoted, each move up becomes significantly more demanding and, therefore, riskier for both the individual and the organization. Senior people fail for many reasons. Their ambition often exceeds their competence. The outstanding performance that brought them this far sometimes lulls them into complacence about their accountability. In some cases, a person is promoted for her personality and finds that her character isn't up to the test. Some people simply receive an inappropriate assignment, given their skills and talents and experience. Leaders sometimes merely misjudge a person's potential.

As I have said elsewhere, a real mystery surrounds human potential and selecting the right person for a difficult job. On one hand, someone's performance often far exceeds our expectations. On the other, as a friend of mine says, "He's got a great pedigree, but he don't hunt."

I would like to make some observations about selecting senior people. I'm convinced that leaders make a fundamental error when they rationalize in their minds the selection of mediocre performers for senior positions. As a way of composing voice and touch, let's think about selecting senior people first in terms of what leaders owe the candidate. By emphasizing the candidate's needs, I think we will significantly improve our chances of ensuring the future of the organization.

Remembering the needs of the organization comes naturally; I'm not worried about a leader's forgetting them. Rather, in a process like this, it's essential that we offer candidates the chance to act on their own behalf. (As you think about selecting senior people, you may want to glance at "What's Fragile?")

Leaders owe it to candidates for senior positions to:

Ask the candidate, "What is it that you will uniquely bring to this organization and to this senior responsibility?" The answer is surely one of the things a candidate should submit in writing. A leader will be on the lookout for several things in the answer. What does the candidate think about heterogeneity in your organization? What are her thoughts on equity and on leading through serving? What does she say about her own level of energy and about her willingness to take risks? Do her written comments convince you that she actually understands the institutional values and culture? What does she say about some of the ideas in the chapter "God's Mix"? What does she say about the competence, contribution, and commitment she will bring to your organization—both personally and professionally?

I'm reminded of an incident involving Secretary of State George Shultz and the Iran-Contra investigations. One of the senators asked the secretary what we should learn from this affair. Shultz replied: "Never give great responsibility to someone who can't live without it."

Establish relevant criteria. We sometimes don't do well in this business of selecting and nurturing senior people because we have silent, irrelevant criteria in mind. Remarks like "He isn't tough enough" or "She isn't old enough" or "He doesn't look right to me" are simply out-of-date, irrelevant, and sometimes illegal. It is a sign of the value of thinking like this that it is seldom written down. Skewed notions about picking people for senior positions abound, but the fact is that today we can bring an entirely new way of thinking to the process of selecting senior people that didn't exist twenty years ago. Just as we cannot run the finances of organizations according to the tax laws of the 1970s, we cannot select senior people solely according to received wisdom.

Give the candidate a clear statement of expectations. This is in addition to criteria and a job outline. In selecting people for senior positions, a leader needs to know how the candidate looks at the organization's values and mission and strategy. A candidate should have a chance to scrutinize a statement of expectations and react candidly to it.

Discuss whether or not the candidate is capable of following her predecessor.

Clarify what about the candidate's performance will be measured. There should be no mystery as to what will constitute acceptable performance and accountability.

Arrange for interviews with people from several levels in the organization. People who work in the plant make excellent interviewers for some senior positions.

Pave the way for new people or people who are to be promoted. Leaders need to prepare the organization for new people to take on the responsibilities of their positions, to prepare the organization to accept and help and nurture people who are to be newly challenged. This begins, of course, when a leader can embrace change, new inputs, and new styles.

Give the candidate opportunities to withdraw gracefully. It may be that a candidate will realize that the position is not for her. Doing the right thing here is important to the organization and even more crucial to the candidate and her family.

Throughout the process of selecting senior people, it seems to me, leaders will be alert to several things. We occasionally have a problem with candidates who temporarily adopt the values of an institution and subsequently try to alter them to resemble their former way of working. On one hand, signs of such an attitude should raise a yellow caution flag for leaders. On the other, we are far more likely to sin in the other direction and fail to pave the way for the necessary and constructive change new leaders often bring to organizations.

In interviews with senior people, pay attention to pronouns. Listen carefully to the candidate's language. Does the "I" keep appearing? In the case of senior leaders, that's a red flag. Listen for the ability to communicate. Listen for spontaneity.

What does the candidate do in the nonprofit sector? Does she serve others and lead without power? What does she read? How does she maintain emotional and intellectual health? What is she curious about?

Once I interviewed a man who seemed to have all the credentials. (As it turned out, he also had very little credibility.) In the course of the conversation, he told me that he had lived for some months in London, for years one of my favorite places and the most exciting large city. Eagerly, I asked him to tell me about London. He answered succinctly: "It's the most central location in Europe if you're seeking to establish distribution."

Not a word about history or museums or theater or architecture or parks or people.

You may want to end the discussion with two simple questions:

- Does this college (or church or business) need you?

- Do you need this college?

After you select a senior leader, the congratulations given and commitments made, there is one more step you may want to consider. Senior leaders have difficult jobs to do; we share a high rate of failure. I'd suggest that you bring it up.

Ask the questions: "If together you and I fail, how would you prefer to deal with it? Would you like to be transferred to another position in the company? Would you like a quiet six months to search for a new job and then resign? Would you prefer to be fired?" This kind of discussion, in my experience, lays the groundwork for open and relaxed talk about performance. As I've said, being promoted to a senior position is a risky business.

Candid talk about failure makes the risk easier to live with.

Do leaders have a future? Yes. But it is a future filled with risk and uncertainty. Does your institution have a future? I certainly hope so. But I'm willing to guarantee you that the quality of that future depends on the senior people you are selecting in the present.

The Attributes of Leadership: A Checklist

.....

I arrived at the local tennis club just after a group of high school students had vacated the locker room. Like chickens, they had not bothered to pick up after themselves. Without thinking too much about it, I gathered up all their towels and put them in a hamper. A friend of mine quietly watched me do this and then asked me a question that I've pondered many times over the years. "Do you pick up towels because you're the president of a company, or are you the president because you pick up towels?"

Leadership, as I said at the beginning of this book, is a serious meddling in the lives of others. Besides picking up towels, what other traits or attributes qualify us to accept the job of leadership?

Some of my friends call me a man of many lists. If you have read this far, you'll probably agree. Here is a list that may help you coalesce your thinking about the good work of leadership. In spite of my admiration for lists, to catalog the attributes of a leader is like fighting the Hydra. Like Hercules, I confront two more heads every time I write one off. In examining one aspect of leadership, I soon discover that I think of something else equally important. Just another proof that leadership is something we never completely understand.

Other people have made lists about leadership. A good one is "The Tasks of Leadership," a chapter in John Gardner's book *On Leadership*. I find that a list brings a sort of discipline to my thinking, and I look at a good list as a musical score. Before it really comes to life, it must be interpreted and performed. How that is accomplished or how you use a list is more up to you than to me.

Above all, leadership is a position of servanthood. Leadership is also a posture of debt; it is a forfeiture of rights. You see! One quality of leadership always implies another. Where does one stop? Here is my list. See what you think.

Integrity. Integrity is the linchpin of leadership. Where integrity is at stake, the leader works publicly. Behavior is the only score that's kept. Lose integrity, and a leader will suddenly find herself in a directionless organization going nowhere.

Vulnerability. Vulnerability is the opposite of self-expression. Vulnerable leaders trust in the abilities of other people; vulnerable leaders allow the people who follow them to do their best. An invulnerable leader can be only as good as her own performance—what a terrifying thought! One caveat: Remember that there is no such thing as safe vulnerability.

Discernment. You cannot buy discernment; you can find it. Discernment lies somewhere between wisdom and judgment. Leaders are required to see many things—pain, beauty, anxiety, loneliness, and heartbreak. Two elements to keep your eye on: the detection of nuance and the perception of changing realities. What kind of antennae do you have?

Awareness of the human spirit. In a special way, all the qualities of a good leader stem from this one. Without understanding the cares, yearnings, and struggles of the human spirit, how could anyone presume to lead a group of people across the street? In modern organizational jargon, person skills always precede professional skills.

221

Courage in relationships. Followers expect a leader to face up to tough decisions. When conflict must be resolved, when justice must be defined and carried out, when promises need to be kept, when the organization needs to hear who counts—these are the times when leaders act with ruthless honesty and live up to their covenant with the people they lead.

Sense of humor. Sometimes the best humor is deadly serious. I've often wondered why. Part of the reason must be that a compassionate sense of humor requires a broad perspective on the human condition, an accounting for many points of view. Surely true leaders have it. You'll find a sense of humor essential to living with ambiguity.

Intellectual energy and curiosity. When you are fortunate enough to lead a group of people, opportunities arise constantly to learn from those people. The very complexity of life today has turned decision making into a process of learning and discovery requiring great intellectual vigor of leaders. We cannot make good decisions unless we accept the responsibility for learning frantically the things that produce them. If you are intent on learning frantically, you actively seek out what followers can teach. And when you seek out the competence of your followers, you begin to enable them to fulfill their potential. When followers are allowed to do their best, they make leadership infinitely easier, and you're free to learn even more. A wonderful cycle, don't you think?

Respect for the future, regard for the present, understanding of the past. Leaders move constantly back and forth between the present and the future. Our perception of each becomes clear and valid if we understand the past. The future requires our humility in the face of all we cannot control. The present requires attention to all the people to whom we are accountable. The past gives us the opportunity to build on the work of our elders.

Predictability. To their followers, leaders owe predictability as a human being. This differs from predictability in strategic planning or decision making, something leaders also should pursue. Leaders must be calculable forces in organizations; they are not free to follow a whim. For example, since leaders are especially responsible for the vision and values of an organization, I would grieve over an unpredictable tender of a group's birthright and future. Something to keep in mind here: Tending a vision is as difficult as conceiving one.

Breadth. A vision of what an organization can become has room for all contributions from all quarters. To borrow from Walt Whitman, leaders are people large enough to contain multitudes.

Comfort with ambiguity. "Leader" is not always a position. Whatever one's position, the amount of ambiguity involved is directly proportional to the amount of leadership required. Healthy organizations exhibit a degree of chaos. A leader will make some sense of it. The more comfortable you can make yourself with ambiguity, the better a leader you will be. Organizations always delegate the job of dealing constructively with ambiguity to their leaders.

Presence. I think that the ability to stop is an important trait of leaders. Many large manufacturing plants have a fleet of bicycles that allow people to save time on trips to various areas of the facility. Such is the case at Herman Miller, but we have placed a restriction on the use of our bicycles. No supervisor may ride one. The reason is simple: You can't have a conversation or ask a question from a bicycle. You can't tap a person going by on a bicycle on the shoulder and say, "Could I talk to you a minute?" Leaders stop—to ask and answer questions, to be patient, to listen to problems, to seek the nuance, to follow up a lead. Leaders quietly and openly wait for the information, good and bad, that enables them to lead.

* * *

I hope this list has both pricked your thinking about leadership and opened you to the potential of leaders. Perhaps one need remember no more than what a friend of mine once said to me. "Leaders stand alone, take the heat, bear the pain, tell the truth." I am constantly excited by what there is to learn!

Epilogue

.....

In the late fourteenth century, the members of New College, at Oxford, moved into their quadrangle, the first structure of its kind, intended to provide for the residents all that they needed. On the north side of the quadrangle sit the chapel and the great hall, beautiful buildings and, as you might imagine, the focus of the life of the college.

In the middle of the nineteenth century, almost five hundred years later, the college hired architect Sir Gilbert Scott to restore the roof of the hall. The roof and the great oak beams that supported it had badly rotted. And so representatives from the college with Sir Gilbert visited Great Hall Woods, in Berkshire, where they expected to find trees for replacement beams. Sure enough, the replacements were standing there, waiting to be hewn out of the living oak trees planted a century before for just that purpose.

An anonymous leader's promise had been fulfilled. The voice and touch of a distant leader had been joined.